Microsoft System Center Endpoint Protection Cookbook

Second Edition

Over 31 simple yet incredibly effective recipes for installing and managing System Center 2016 Endpoint Protection

Nicolai Henriksen

BIRMINGHAM - MUMBAI

Microsoft System Center Endpoint Protection Cookbook

Second Edition

First published: October 2012

Second edition: December 2016

Production reference: 1151216

Published by Packt Publishing Ltd.
Livery Place
35 Livery Street
Birmingham B3 2PB, UK.

ISBN 978-1-78646-428-6

www.packtpub.com

Credits

Author
Nicolai Henriksen

Reviewer
Ronni Pedersen

Commissioning Editor
Kartikey Pandey

Acquisition Editor
Prachi Bisht

Content Development Editor
Abhishek Jadhav

Technical Editor
Aditya Khadye

Copy Editors
Safis Editing
Dipti Mankame

Project Coordinator
Judie Jose

Proofreader
Safis Editing

Indexer
Pratik Shirodkar

Graphics
Kirk D'Penha

Production Coordinator
Shantanu N. Zagade

Cover Work
Shantanu N. Zagade

About the Author

Nicolai Henriksen works as a chief technical architect consultant presently and lives in Bergen, Norway, with his wife and three children.

He has worked in the information technology consulting business for almost two decades, working and implementing systems in all kinds of various businesses from small to enterprises, mostly with products within the Microsoft family. But he has gained great experience and knowledge about many vendors and products.

Nicolai's educational background started with electronic engineering, and he worked for a while as a technician. That has also been his great interest, besides computers.

He started exploring computers in 1980 as a teenager and somehow then understood the meaning and future perspective that computer science had for the world.

For the past 12 years, he has been dedicatedly working with System Center Configuration Manager in customer projects. Since 2012, Endpoint Protection got integrated into this great product and Nicolai says that by then the amount of companies using this product has increased enormously.

Since 1990, when malware and computer viruses started to evolve, he started helping business to protect their computers with all kinds of antimalware products.

This is the first book Nicolai has written, yet he has done several reviews on System Center books in the past couple of years, and has thought of writing a book for quite some time. It's not unlikely that we will see more books from Nicolai in the future.

Nicolai also speaks in public conferences while he loves to teach and share his knowledge with others. The fact that people are willing to listen and you have burning desire to share without demanding anything back gives a great feeling according to him. He spends some time blogging, Twittering, and answering questions on Technet forums.

In 2012, Nicolai was awarded the Microsoft Most Valuable Professional (MVP), which only a few people in the world have achieved. He then specialized in the popular and great management product called System Center Configuration Manager.

Nicolai has been balancing a life as a family man with intense creativity and passion within computer science for many years.

Acknowledgment

I would like to thank my wife, Kristina, for putting up with my many late night working, and our children, Tuva, Malin, and Olav for being patient and kind to their dad. The love and care from these important persons in my life have been essential for my work and career. And I want to thank Packt Publishing for giving me the opportunity to write this book. I would also like to thank the Microsoft MVP Program and MVP members for all the support and inspiration, and MVP Ronni Pedersen for doing a good job reviewing this book. Finally, I want to thank my mom and dad, Ella and Eigil, for always being there for me.

About the Reviewer

Ronni Pedersen works as a Cloud solution architect, Microsoft Enterprise Mobility MVP, Certified Trainer, event speaker, and author. Today, he works for EG A/S, where he also contributes to the community by writing articles and sharing tips and tricks on `http://www.ronnipedersen.com/`. In recent years, he has been invited as a speaker at various international conferences and User Groups meetings, such as TechEd, Microsoft Management Summit, Midwest Management Summit, Microsoft Ignite, TechTalks, and the global Microsoft Cloud Roadshow. In 2008, he was one of the cofounders of the Danish System Center User Group.

www.PacktPub.com

eBooks, discount offers, and more

Did you know that Packt offers eBook versions of every book published, with PDF and ePub files available? You can upgrade to the eBook version at www.PacktPub.com and as a print book customer, you are entitled to a discount on the eBook copy. Get in touch with us at customercare@packtpub.com for more details.

At www.PacktPub.com, you can also read a collection of free technical articles, sign up for a range of free newsletters and receive exclusive discounts and offers on Packt books and eBooks.

https://www.packtpub.com/mapt

Get the most in-demand software skills with Mapt. Mapt gives you full access to all Packt books and video courses, as well as industry-leading tools to help you plan your personal development and advance your career.

Why subscribe?

- ► Fully searchable across every book published by Packt
- ► Copy and paste, print, and bookmark content
- ► On demand and accessible via a web browser

Instant updates on new Packt books

Get notified! Find out when new books are published by following @PacktEnterprise on Twitter or the *Packt Enterprise* Facebook page.

Table of Contents

Preface

System Center Endpoint Protection, or Windows Defender, is a great security product when using System Center Configuration Manager or Microsoft Intune.

Its ability to protect computers in business increases every day, and it continually improves its features to meet today's security risks and attacks.

Because over 75% of all business around the world are now using the popular and great management tool System Center Configuration Manager, Endpoint Protection has also become widespread over that past few years.

In this book, we will explore the main motivation of using the well-known and established System Center Endpoint Protection and Windows Defender. You will gain knowledge about how to set up and configure the products for your organization based on real-life experience and best practices from a field expert and Microsoft Most Valuable Professional. Throughout the book, you will see several best practice tips and recipes for you to use in your daily life as a security administrator.

This book is suitable for everyone who works with computers, but especially useful for IT administrators who work with System Center Configuration Manager, Endpoint Protection, and Intune.

The book will be useful for most kinds of businesses, from small to large, with making decisions, whether they are already using the product or just considering it. And there will be some recipes of value to you even if you are not using Endpoint Protection or Windows Defender.

Either way, reading this book will give you value that you can take with you in the future. Windows Defender comes built in with Windows 10 as well as Windows Server 2016 and you need to decide whether you choose to use it or disable it.

You will also gain deeper knowledge as a System Center Configuration Manager admin of how to handle and administrate the Endpoint Protection role to suite your antimalware admin needs, and also perhaps give you some good tips regarding Configuration Manager.

What this book covers

Chapter 1, *Planning and Getting Started with System Center Endpoint Protection*, walks you through an easy approach to what you need to consider when planning and designing an System Center Configuration Manner hierarchy with the Endpoint Protection in mind. You will gain knowledge of real-life best practices when setting up SCCM.

Chapter 2, *Configuring Endpoint Protection in Configuration Manager*, walks through all the necessary steps to configure SCCM with Endpoint Protection environment, how to configure Definition Updates, and shows how to run it successfully along with SCCM and WSUS.

Chapter 3, *Operations and Maintenance for Endpoint Protection in Configuration Manager*, describes the workflow of creation and deploying antimalware policies using SCCM. The chapter also shows how to configure Windows Firewall and monitor the Endpoint Protection clients.

Chapter 4, *Updates*, dives into advanced and crucial Endpoint Protection update functionalities. This chapter also covers the different supported ways of handling updates, as well as taking in to consideration working with low bandwidth-connected branch offices.

Chapter 5, *Security and Privacy for Endpoint Protection in Configuration Manager*, focuses on security and privacy concerning SCCM and Endpoint Protection, with some best practices. It gives also the opportunity gain knowledge of Microsoft Security Center with Automatic Sample submission.

Chapter 6, *Configuring and Troubleshooting Performance and Advanced Protection*, discusses what to consider when thinking of safety and making applications work properly with the antimalware solution and recipes on how to handle OS deployment and BitLocker.

Chapter 7, *Troubleshooting and Fixing Issues*, provides best practices to troubleshoot SCCM with a focus on Endpoint Protection when it generates errors during its setup and utilization. It starts by tackling major issues presented in SCCM that reflect many other components and explains how to escalate problem resolution using debugging tools and hands-on tips.

Chapter 8, *Malware Handling*, the best chapter, comes last in this book and provides real-life experience of handling malware with a focus on Endpoint Protection. But in this chapter, you will also gain valuable knowledge about how you can improve your security even more and protect against ransomware.

What you need for this book

This book assumes a medium-level of System Center Configuration Manager knowledge, basic knowledge of Windows Workstation, and moderate experience with Windows Server. The book will go through simply toward a more advanced SCCM environment, which may require a basic understanding of networking and virtualization concepts. As this is a cookbook, there will be several recipes that you can try out and benefit from using in your production environment after testing that they work in your business.

With the Microsoft-wide evaluation licence, you will be able to try this product for 180 days.

SCCM can be installed and run either on a bare metal or virtual machine. However, this book requires that you have enough resources to the whole setup. Minimum hardware or virtual requirements are as follows:

- CPU: 2 cores
- Memory: 8 GB RAM
- Disk space: 80 GB

In this book, you will need the following software list:

- Microsoft Windows Server
- Microsoft SQL Server
- Microsoft Windows Assessment and Deployment Kit ADK
- Microsoft System Center Configuration Manager (SCCM)

Internet connectivity is required to install the necessary to get all the setup updates during installation. Although it can be predownloaded, you will need Internet connectivity to get the WSUS and Software Update Point working.

Who this book is for

To make use of the content of this book, basic prior knowledge of SCCM as well as handling Windows is expected. If you do not have this knowledge, it is always possible to catch up the basic requirements by having a quick read of the major components of the Microsoft Technet. Refer to the following link: `https://docs.microsoft.com/nb-no/sccm/core/servers/deploy/start-using`.

There are several books about SCCM and online guides that can improve your knowledge of the product. As SCCM is a huge product, I recommend you start with the basics first so that you have a good foundation and understanding of how it all works.

But this book will also explain very well all the terminology and recipes so that you can actually understand them with very little experience in advance.

This book is well-suited for antivirus and antimalware administrators, as well as security administrators, to gain more understanding and knowledge of how this works. But the book is also highly valuable for SCCM admins to understand the needs for security admins.

And even if you are not at all interested in System Center Endpoint Protection or Windows Defender, as an admin, you feel a security responsibility to keep up with today's threats and how you can protect your business computers even more. There is information and recipes regarding how to protect against ransomware.

Sections

In this book, you will find several headings that appear frequently (Getting ready, How to do it, How it works, There's more, and See also).

To give clear instructions on how to complete a recipe, we use these sections as follows:

Getting ready

This section tells you what to expect in the recipe and describes how to set up any software or any preliminary settings required for the recipe.

How to do it...

This section contains the steps required to follow the recipe.

How it works...

This section usually consists of a detailed explanation of what happened in the previous section.

There's more...

This section consists of additional information about the recipe in order to make the reader more knowledgeable about the recipe.

See also

This section provides helpful links to other useful information for the recipe.

Conventions

In this book, you will find a number of text styles that distinguish between different kinds of information. Here are some examples of these styles and an explanation of their meaning.

Code words in text, database table names, folder names, filenames, file extensions, pathnames, dummy URLs, user input, and Twitter handles are shown as follows: "You need to make a package of the `scepinstall.exe` with the policy file."

Any command-line input or output is written as follows:

```
New-FsrmFileScreen -Path "$i" -Active: $true -IncludeGroup "CryptoWall"
-Notification $Notification
}
------------
```

New terms and **important words** are shown in bold. Words that you see on the screen, for example, in menus or dialog boxes, appear in the text like this: "I recommend putting its database to the full **SQL Server** and not **Internal Database**"

Warnings or important notes appear in a box like this.

Tips and tricks appear like this.

Reader feedback

Feedback from our readers is always welcome. Let us know what you think about this book—what you liked or disliked. Reader feedback is important for us as it helps us develop titles that you will really get the most out of.

To send us general feedback, simply e-mail feedback@packtpub.com, and mention the book's title in the subject of your message.

If there is a topic that you have expertise in and you are interested in either writing or contributing to a book, see our author guide at www.packtpub.com/authors.

Customer support

Now that you are the proud owner of a Packt book, we have a number of things to help you to get the most from your purchase.

Downloading the color images of this book

We also provide you with a PDF file that has color images of the screenshots/diagrams used in this book. The color images will help you better understand the changes in the output. You can download this file from `https://www.packtpub.com/sites/default/files/downloads/MicrosoftSystemCenterEndpointProtectionCookbook_ColorImages.pdf`

Errata

Although we have taken every care to ensure the accuracy of our content, mistakes do happen. If you find a mistake in one of our books—maybe a mistake in the text or the code—we would be grateful if you could report this to us. By doing so, you can save other readers from frustration and help us improve subsequent versions of this book. If you find any errata, please report them by visiting `http://www.packtpub.com/submit-errata`, selecting your book, clicking on the **Errata Submission Form** link, and entering the details of your errata. Once your errata are verified, your submission will be accepted and the errata will be uploaded to our website or added to any list of existing errata under the Errata section of that title.

To view the previously submitted errata, go to `https://www.packtpub.com/books/content/support` and enter the name of the book in the search field. The required information will appear under the **Errata** section.

Piracy

Piracy of copyrighted material on the Internet is an ongoing problem across all media. At Packt, we take the protection of our copyright and licenses very seriously. If you come across any illegal copies of our works in any form on the Internet, please provide us with the location address or website name immediately so that we can pursue a remedy.

Please contact us at `copyright@packtpub.com` with a link to the suspected pirated material.

We appreciate your help in protecting our authors and our ability to bring you valuable content.

Questions

If you have a problem with any aspect of this book, you can contact us at `questions@packtpub.com`, and we will do our best to address the problem.

1
Planning and Getting Started with System Center Endpoint Protection

In this chapter, we will cover the following recipes:

▶ How does Endpoint Protection in Configuration Manager work

▶ Planning for Endpoint Protection

▶ Prerequisites of the infrastructure

▶ Best practices for Endpoint Protection in Configuration Manager

▶ Administrating workflow for Endpoint Protection in Configuration Manager

Introduction

System Center Endpoint Protection is Microsoft's antimalware product for small, large, and enterprise businesses.

It is not a free product, so you do need to be licensed to install and manage your clients with **System Center Configuration Manager** (**SCCM**) or **Intune**. It's very easy to set up and manage in both management systems, but **Configuration Manager** has more advanced features when it comes to policy configuring and adapting the antimalware product for your workstations and servers.

Endpoint Protection can also be installed on Mac OSX. Since SCCM also has a client agent for Mac OSX, you have a complete antimalware solution to handle and protect your Mac machines too. It's important not to forget this option, as incidents of attacks and malware keep rising on that platform as well. There is also Endpoint Protection support for Linux now.

If or when you're running in Microsoft Azure you now have the ability to enable Microsoft Endpoint Protection on your virtual machines or services running in Azure. Just a few clicks away, using some neat PowerShell scripts, you have the ability to enable and configure Endpoint Protection throughout the whole server park on several servers.

Microsoft has done a pretty good job on their antimalware product with System Center Endpoint Protection, and continues to improve greatly.

In my opinion, for over almost a decade (since back in the days when it was called **Forefront**) it has proven to be a worthy competitor to other well-known security, anti-virus and antimalware products on the market. I've worked with most of them and seen them in action. It strikes me that System Center Endpoint Protection works fast and effortlessly with minimum impact on the system compared to others. It is important to mention it has never let me or any of my customers down when it comes to handling malware. However, of course, if an administrator is very careless, they could easily get some nasty piece of software installed. The product has come a long way and is constantly improving. It is slightly false positive and is pretty good in proactive detection of unknown and mutated malware code. This is very important today, as that is the one thing hijackers and malware code writers usually do to try to hide or escape from security products.

Versioning in System Center Configuration Manager is new.

The **1511** build is the first and the base build of the new Configuration Manager platform. Microsoft will not brand it the 2016 version, because this will be continuously updated over the years to come with new builds, with the *first two digits indicating the year and the second two the month it's released*.

1602 is the latest baseline version you can install at the moment when setting up a new System Center Configuration Manager hierarchy in your business. From there you can upgrade from within the console pretty easily to the next version available through the update channel.

With each new build upgrade it's very likely there will be improvements and new features regarding Endpoint Protection as well. So it's even more important to keep your SCCM environment up-to-date when you have that role established.

How does Endpoint Protection in Configuration Manager work

This will give you a good understanding as to how Endpoint Protection in Configuration Manager works, so that you will have a better understanding when you deploy and manage this in your environment.

Endpoint Protection together with Configuration Manager is a pretty powerful solution and you need to get it right so the harm done is minimum. The better solution you provide, and the better the job you do, the more proactive and productive your co-workers will be.

How to do it...

System Center Endpoint Protection is not a standalone product; it is integrated into the popular and great management and deployment product called SCCM, it's a dedicated role and the installation binary lies among the Configuration Manager client installation files. So you need both the System Center Configuration Manager Client and System Center Endpoint Protection to make this work. This provides great benefits when it comes to control, deployment and monitoring of the antimalware software in your organization. Every anti-virus or antimalware product needs a management client or module that can handle downloading and installation, and control and handle different actions to make sure that the antimalware product itself is operating as it should.

System Center Endpoint Protection has no built-in or dedicated management module of its own, so it is designed to be managed as well as licensed through the System Center Configuration Manager or Microsoft Intune.

Microsoft has always been good at making use of technology that's already available, and for the most part this gives more advantages than drawbacks. Every antimalware product needs a management client to monitor, set policies, deploy and update their product. Microsoft has not created a separate management agent for their Endpoint Protection because they had one already with SCCM. Given that it's being used today by approximately 70% of all businesses on the planet, it was an easy choice. So they made it work together with all the features in the same console that you use to manage your workstations, servers and devices. With this, you save resources such as processing and memory on your client as well as on the server side, and it simplifies management too. In most cases, businesses save money on their licenses as well, since they are already licensed to run this.

This is what the client GUI looks like. It's very smooth, clean, and easy to use, and gives clear indications if something is wrong. *Green* is good and *Red* is bad.

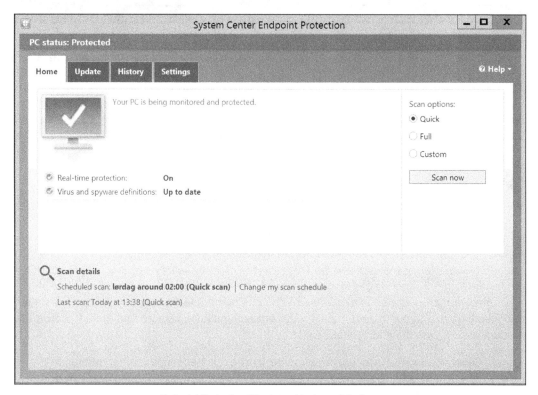

Endpoint Protection Client graphical user interface

For definition and engine updates it uses Windows Update with Microsoft's own definitions, so there is no need for any extra download components to make it work. This also has the benefit that it will be coordinated with other Windows Update installations so they don't encounter any conflicts during installation. Windows Update fetches the updates from either a local **Windows Server Update Services (WSUS)** or by SCCM. If it cannot reach those it will continue, after a given amount of time, to download it over the Internet directly from Microsoft.

With the use of Configuration Manager to handle Endpoint Protection, it will give you the following benefits as mentioned on `http://slothx.net/wiki/SC2012_ConfigMgr_ PDFDownload.pdf`:

- ▶ Remediation of malware and spyware.
- ▶ Remediation of rootkit detection.
- ▶ Remediation of potentially unwanted software (this is a new feature in version 1602 of SCCM).

- ▶ Assessment of critical vulnerability with automatic updates of definition and engine.

- ▶ Network Inspection System vulnerability detection.

- ▶ Malware reported directly through Microsoft Active Protection Services. When you join and enable this service, it will trigger the client to download the latest definitions from the Malware Protection Center when unidentified malware is detected on a computer.

System Center Endpoint Protection has another nice feature when running virtualized environments, as many do these days: if you want to preserve disk IO as well as excessive CPU usage while antimalware is doing its scheduled scanning, you can set System Center Endpoint Protection to randomize the scanning start time so that they do not occur simultaneously on all guest machines that are hosted by the server.

Windows 10 is now supported (from version System Configuration Manager 2012 SP2), and we will cover that in more detail later in the book. SCCM manages Defender, which comes with Windows 10, and which is basically the same as Endpoint Protection.

What made Endpoint Protection that good

In my opinion, Microsoft made some very good investments over a large period of time. They launched a free antimalware product called Microsoft Security Essentials back in 2009-2010. The beta release was installed on millions of home computers, and boy did it did detect a lot of different kinds of malware. Many of the computers had not been protected for a long period of time because their previous antimalware product had expired, often the trial version that came installed with Windows when they bought it, and which was not working right or had not been updated for some reason. So Security Essentials had a couple of years to toughen up, so to say, and get stronger by learning what to deal with around the world. The users were happy; they got a free antimalware product that was getting better and better day by day.

The other aspect that has a huge impact on how well Endpoint Protection is working and how they got it to run so smoothly is that Microsoft has great knowledge of their own products. They know all the bits and pieces of how the operating system works and most of the applications that run on every machine and server on the planet. They have a very large Security Response Network Cloud Center that monitors all threats within a split second around the world and can instantly take action in the case of a massive outbreak.

Planning for the Endpoint Protection

Put on an architect's hat and let's see how to implement the Endpoint Protection role in your business.

Often there are actually very few considerations when you need to implement and engage Endpoint Protection in your business, especially if you already have Configuration Manager or Intune installed. There are a couple of important topics to understand in the planning phase: as in what do I need to consider, and why? Endpoint Protection utilizes the Configuration Manager client to transport the policies and actions it requires. That part of the operation flows very smoothly though the existing Configuration Manager hierarchy you are most likely to have set up. The heavy part regarding bandwidth utilization would be the definition package and engine update, depending on whether you already have a well-structured and organized software update point role in place or not, as the software will update two or three times a day. Then it needs to deliver these packages and transport them to the Distribution Point servers in your hierarchy. There are therefore a few things to consider. You will find more information and tips about some of these settings in further chapters of this book.

How to do it...

First of all, it's for sure that you cannot have two antimalware products running on your workstations or servers. If that happens, you are likely to crash the operating system and, worst case, it won't start up again other than by booting in safe mode. If that's the case, you would have a huge job ahead of you because this would involve a manual approach to handle every machine.

Now that would be a worst case scenario, and in my experience it never happens because you plan, test and deploy in a controlled matter. Luckily, Microsoft has put in an automatic detection of a few other antimalware products and a fully automatic removal of those products as best it can. It is working pretty well in my experience, but I would rather use it as a fail-safe mechanism if your own removal plan should fail.

The current list of products that Microsoft will try to remove if they exist on any machine you're deploying Endpoint Protection to can be found at `https://technet.microsoft.com/en-us/library/gg682067.aspx#BKMK_EndpointProtectionDeviceSettings`.

- ▶ Symantec Antivirus Corporate Edition version 10
- ▶ Symantec Endpoint Protection version 11
- ▶ Symantec Endpoint Protection Small Business Edition version 12
- ▶ McAfee VirusScan Enterprise version 8
- ▶ Trend Micro OfficeScan
- ▶ Microsoft Forefront Codename Stirling Beta 2
- ▶ Microsoft Forefront Codename Stirling Beta 3
- ▶ Microsoft Forefront Client Security v1
- ▶ Microsoft Security Essentials v1
- ▶ Microsoft Security Essentials 2010

- ▶ Microsoft Forefront Endpoint Protection 2010
- ▶ Microsoft Security Center Online v1

This automatic uninstall setting is located in the client setting of the Configuration Manager and is turned ON by default when Enabling Endpoint Protection.

However, I encourage you to do some research in your organization, about what products are in use right now. It might be more than you might think; most people are in for a surprise or two on what's running, especially on the workstations. Most likely you will have a handful of different antimalware software running, so you need to do some digging around, and once you have a Configuration Manager with a full inventory of all your clients' antimalware software, that's not a big problem. You just need to have some knowledge about what to look for. When you have identified the different products, you need to plan how to uninstall and get rid of them in a safe way, whilst at the same time keeping the machine secure, since you don't want to leave the machine unprotected.

Secondly, you need to ensure that Endpoint Protection will be able to get updates. Now this is very important, and you have some options that may have an impact depending on what your network infrastructure looks like. Do you have many remote locations, do you have satellite connections, and do your laptops travel a lot?

The Endpoint Protection role needs to be installed on your **Central Administration Site (CAS)** if you have one, and it needs to be installed on your Primary Site servers as well.

In the following graphic you can see different scenarios with a CAS Central Administration Site Server on top, then a **Primary Site** followed by a **Secondary Site**. Following that, you might even have dedicated **Distribution Points** servers to smaller locations or clients. **Secondary Sites** are generally fading out unless you have very large branch offices or locations with several thousand clients. However, the scenario following is for very large businesses that need redundancy and security.

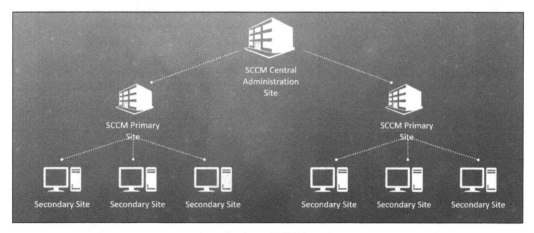

Large business SCCM hierarchy

The hierarchy for most businesses, where you have a **Primary Site** server on top and a **Distribution Point** server following placed at branch offices or locations around the world, is shown in the following figure:

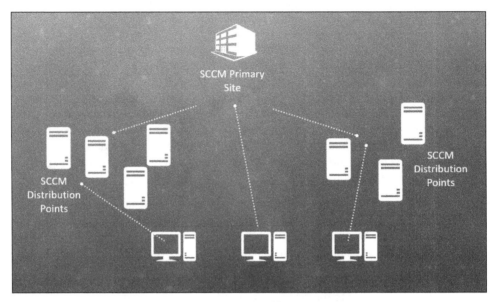

Conventional business SCCM hierarchy

You can see a simple illustration of how **Intune** work in the following figure. Every client talks directly over the **Internet** to **Azure** in the Cloud. It has both upsides and downsides, but requires very little infrastructure and it's easy to maintain:

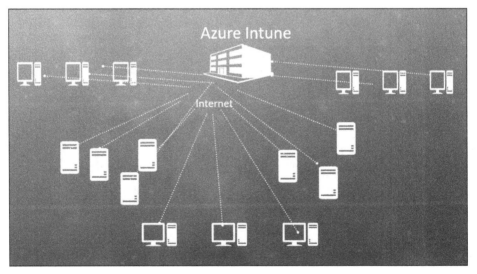

Principal network schematic picture of Microsoft Intune

Prerequisites of the infrastructure

Endpoint Protection in System Center 2012 Configuration Manager has external dependencies and requirements in the product to make it work. This depends somewhat on what platform you're running on, and what your infrastructure and network looks like. You will find some pointers and tips later in this book. Now, you are most likely to have a WSUS in your infrastructure already, but you cannot use this with Configuration Manager. You need to set up a new one, as re-using an existing old WSUS server is not supported nor recommended by Microsoft. SCCM will setup and configure the WSUS with the settings from the Software Update Point role and therefore needs to be a fresh new database and WSUS installation.

Getting ready

First, start the Server Manager on your Windows Server, most likely at your primary site; or on the server that you will be using for the Software Update Point role for the SCCM hierarchy.

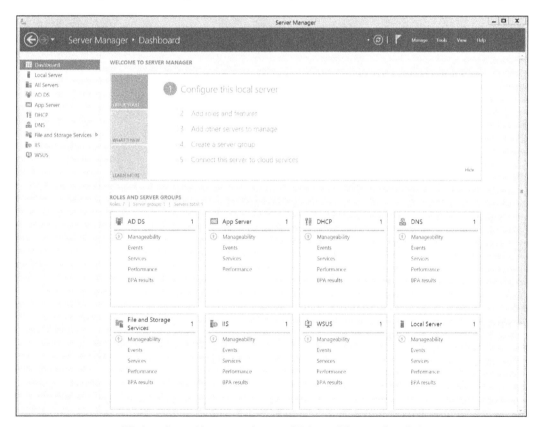

Windows Server Manager and status of Roles and Features Installed

The WSUS role should be installed. I recommend putting its database to the full **SQL Server** and not **Internal Database**. The SQL License is included with SCCM. Make sure **Internal Database** is not selected. You might want to install it as a separate instance on your SQL server for performance monitoring and balancing resources like memory, CPU and disk, but this is not a requirement. Remember to press **Cancel** on the last part of the **Wizard** when it wants you to configure the WSUS products and type of updates. Configuration Manager will take care of that part when setting up the software update role afterwards in Configuration Manager.

When WSUS is installed go into **Configuration Manager Console** and **Administration**.

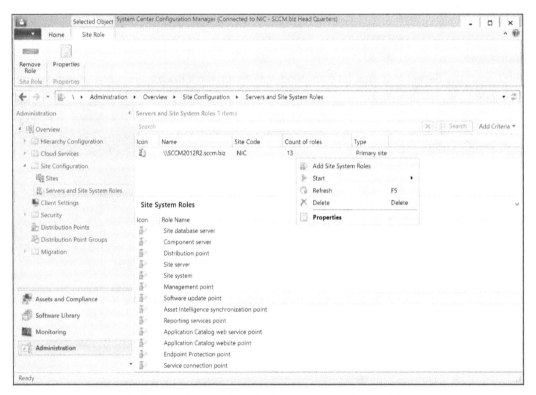

Configuration Manager Console where you add Site System Roles

In **Site Configuration | Servers and Site System Roles** you would right click on the **Server** you want to use as the **Software update point** and click **Add Site System Roles**

From there it's pretty straight forward. Microsoft recommends using port 8530, and the WSUS Role installation in Server Manager suggests you use this. These are also the ports that are default when you're on Windows Server 2012 and 2012 R2. While on Windows Server 2008 and 2008 R2, the default ports are 80 and 443.

So the software update role in Configuration Manager uses and relies on the WSUS role in the Windows Server.

In the next chapter we will go through in more detail how to configure all the settings you need.

How to do it...

Regarding the planning phase, when it comes to Configuration Manager there are some external dependencies.

 Please see the Prerequisites at Microsoft Technet:
`https://technet.microsoft.com/en-us/library/hh508780.aspx`

How it works...

Basically the software update role within Configuration Manager utilizes and uses the WSUS role that comes with the Windows Server.

Best practices for Endpoint Protection in Configuration Manager

Use the following best practices for Endpoint Protection in System Center 2012 Configuration Manager.

How to do it...

It is a good practice in Configuration Manager and all management systems when dealing with deployment to test, test, and test again, given that you want to run changes in a smooth manner with as few surprises and as little noise as possible.

I would also recommend that you create a separate client setting policy that enables and installs Endpoint Protection, and that you deploy to a dedicated collection for this purpose when you start to test and deploy to computers, as the following screenshot will show you.

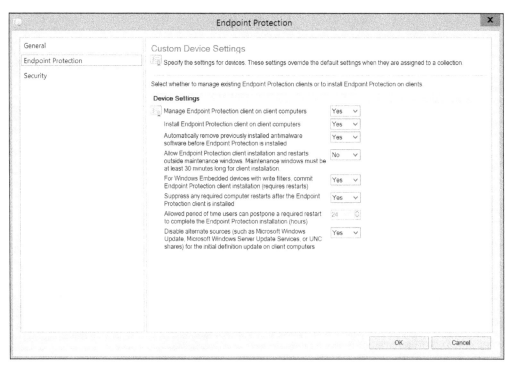

Configuration Manager Client setting where you configure Endpoint Protection Installation settings

The setting on the picture preceding **Disable alternate sources (such as Microsoft Windows Update, Microsoft Windows Server Update Services, or UNC shares) for the initial definition update on client computers** are important to pay attention to. This is enabled by default, because it may have a huge impact on your network. As the initial download of definitions that each client needs right after installation would be around 150MB, you might not want to download it over a low bandwidth connection.

More about this in *Chapter 4, Updates.*

So you have a collection where you've deployed the required definition update and added the client setting that deploys the Endpoint Protection client, you have created and deployed the appropriate Endpoint Protection policies, and you've also deployed to that collection, so you're good to go. Then you can just add more and more computers to that collection and monitor the results over time. I would recommend picking different kinds of computers in your organization to make sure the first phase of the Endpoint Protection deployment captures as many different environments and different users in the early stage as possible. The same method is actually recommended when it comes to software updates on a daily or weekly basis.

Speaking of software updates, it's recommended that you keep definition updates in a separate package that does not contain other software updates. This keeps the size to a minimum and allows replication to distribution points to operate more quickly and efficiently.

Administrating workflow for Endpoint Protection in Configuration Manager

When administrating and working with Endpoint Protection in SCCM you can follow this workflow list to make sure you have everything covered. You will find settings regarding Endpoint Protection in different places in the Configuration Manager Console so that it also makes sense in the management tool. Administrators usually find this easy when they are used to working with Configuration Manager and it gives great benefits and flexibility.

Getting ready

Make sure you have made a plan for your business on how you are going to deploy and manage Endpoint Protection. Also, undertake the required assessment to find what kind of antimalware or antivirus products might be installed on the machines and plan how to handle this.

How to do it...

Use the following workflow as a reference to help you enable, configure, manage and monitor Endpoint Protection in System Center 2012 Configuration Manager Technet link: `https://technet.microsoft.com/en-us/library/hh526775.aspx`.

Now you might have another antimalware product in your environment from before, and you need a solution that can help you replace that. So you need a way to uninstall the product you want to get rid of and install Endpoint Protection in the same process to keep the clients secure. We will cover this more thoroughly in another chapter in this book.

2

Configuring Endpoint Protection in Configuration Manager

In this chapter, we will cover the following recipes:

- ▶ Configuring Endpoint Protection in Configuration Manager
- ▶ Configuring alerts for Endpoint Protection in Configuration Manager
- ▶ Configuring definition updates for Endpoint Protection in Configuration Manager
- ▶ Provisioning the Endpoint Protection Client in a disk image in Configuration Manager

Introduction

In this chapter we will cover all you need to do to configure Endpoint Protection in Configuration Manager.

This is the part where you need to think through every setting you make so that it has the positive impact you want in your organization. Misconfiguration may have a very bad outcome as this has to do with security.

Hopefully you will have a better understanding after reading this chapter.

Configuring Endpoint Protection in Configuration Manager

In order to manage security and malware on your client computers with Endpoint Protection, there are a few steps you must setup and configure in order to get it working in **System Center Configuration Manager (SCCM)**.

Getting ready

In this chapter we assume that you have SCCM in-place and working, and that you have setup and installed the Software Update Point Role with its prerequisites like **Windows Server Update Services (WSUS)**.

We also assume that you have planned and thought through what impact this has in your environment, and have a good understanding of how this should and will work in your Configuration Manager hierarchy.

Later in this chapter we have a topic about configuring definition updates. Please go through that to get some pointers on how you should configure definition updates depending on your kind of environment.

How to do it...

First, we start by installing the Endpoint Protection Role from within the SCCM console. This role must be installed before you can configure and start using Endpoint Protection.

The Endpoint Protection role must only be installed on one site system server, and if you have a **Central Administration Site (CAS)** in your hierarchy the role must be installed there. Most commonly, if you have a stand-alone primary site, you only need to install it there.

Be aware that when you install the Endpoint Protection Role on the site server it will also install the Endpoint Protection client on that same server. This is by default and cannot be changed. However, services and scans are disabled so that you can still run any other existing antimalware solution that you may already have in place. No real-time scanning or any other form of scanning will be performed by Endpoint Protection before you enable it with a policy. Be aware of this so that you don't accidentally enable it while another antimalware solution is installed.

Installing the Endpoint Protection Role is pretty easy and straight forward; these are the steps to manage that:

1. To install and configure Endpoint Protection Role, open the Configuration Manager console, click **Administration**, and in the **Administration** workspace **expand Site Configuration** and click on **Servers** and **Site System Roles**.

2. Click on **Add Site System Roles** as shown in the image following:

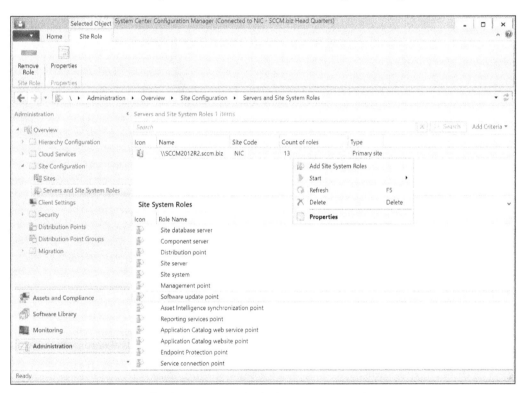

Add Site System Roles in the Configuration Manager Console

3. On the next screen I chose to use the default settings that will use the **server's computer account** to install the role on the chosen server. In my case, I have a single primary site server where all the roles reside and this will require no other preparation. However, keep in mind that if you are adding roles to other site system servers it will require that you add the primary site server's computer **Account** to the local administrators' group, or you could use an installation account as shown in the following screenshot:

Add Site System Roles Wizard

4. Let's click **Next.**

    This is the page where we choose the **Endpoint Protection** Role that we want to install.

    It will only list the roles that you have not already added to the chosen server.

    Notice that it also warns you to have software updates and antimalware definitions already in place and deployed. The warning will appear regardless of whether you have these in place already or not as shown in the next screenshot:

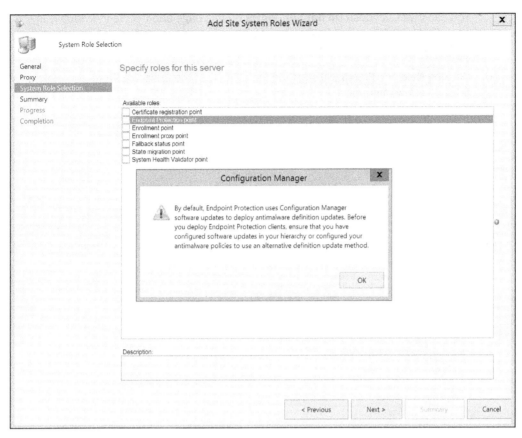

Endpoint Protection setup Wizard

5. The next page on the wizard is about **Microsoft Active Protection Service membership**.

    I like to think of this as the *cloud* feature, and I encourage you to consider setting this to **Advanced membership** as that will give you and Microsoft a greater chance of dealing will any *unknown* types of malware. This will send more information from the infected client about the surroundings of the malware. Then, Microsoft can investigate the bits and pieces more thoroughly in their environment from the cloud service. If it turns out that this is infectious malware, like a Trojan downloader for example, it will get further removal instructions directly and try its best to remove it automatically.

    Now, this feature will work either way that you choose, but it will work even better if you choose to share information. Most other anti-virus and antimalware products don't ask about this, they just enable it, but Microsoft has chosen to let you decide, because there could be situations in which you might not want to share.

You can always choose **Do not join MAPS** on this page and decide individually in each Endpoint Protection Policy how you want it to behave. Setting it here simply makes this the default setting for every policy made afterwards.

6. Clicking **Next >** | **Finish** will start the installation of the Endpoint Protection Role and finish in a few minutes.

Microsoft Active Protection Service setting when installing the Endpoint Protection role

In the **Monitoring | Components status** shown following you can see two components starting with **SMS_ENDPOINT_PROTECTION** that will have a green icon on the left and will tell you that the role is installed.

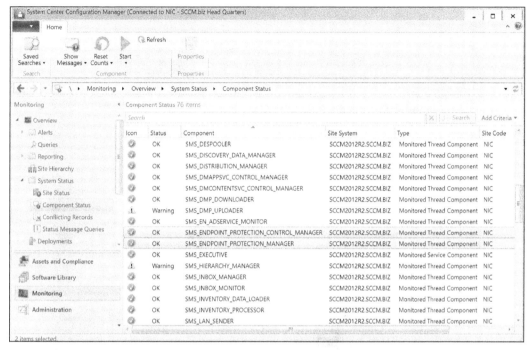

Endpoint Protection roles status in the Configuration Manager Component Status view

How it works...

So, as you can see. Installing the Endpoint Protection role is easy and straightforward when you have done the proper planning and preparation.

However, there is more configuration to do, and this will be covered in the next topic.

If you remember, the Endpoint Protection client will always be installed on the site server that has the Endpoint Protection role installed. By default, it is set with no scanning or real-time protection enabled, and has a red icon on the task-bar on the right side as shown following:

The preceding screenshot shows you the Endpoint Protection client installed but, with **Real-time protection Off** as default when the System Center Endpoint Protection role is installed on a Site System Server.

Configuring alerts for Endpoint Protection in Configuration Manager

You need properly configured alerts that give you exactly what you need to know, especially when it comes to monitoring an antimalware product.

I would think that you don't want emails every minute about all the malware found on every machine in your corporation, so configure it more intelligently and distinguish who needs what information.

For example, an IT Manager might prefer to only get email alerts if there were to be a critical matter like an outbreak on the network, or if, say, the Configuration Manager client check and remediation fails on a certain percentage of all clients. This is important because it's the Configuration Manager client that will be forwarding the alerting message to the Configuration Manager site server. If that client somehow starts to fail for whatever reason, you have a problem to attend as quickly as possible. Malware often tries to disable and strike out antimalware solutions and management solutions in order to be left alone to work privately toward their agenda. So this is information an IT manager should know about if it reaches a critical level.

You will set up configuring alerts for Endpoint Protection in Configuration Manager with the following steps mentioned in the *How to do it...* section.

Getting ready

You need to decide what collection you will be monitoring: All systems, the servers, or just the workstations. What collection did you enable the Endpoint Protection on in the client settings policy?

How to do it...

1. We start by going into **Assets and Compliance | Device Collections**.

   In my situation, I have deployed a client settings policy that enables Endpoint Protection on my collection called **All Windows Workstations**. This is a collection that I have created that will contain all clients with operating system like %**Windows NT Workstation**%.

Configuration Manager Console and the Collection All Windows Workstations

2. Right click the **Collection** you want to set alerting up on and choose **Properties**. The **Alerts** pane will look like this:

All Windows Workstations Properties where you can configure Alerts

3. Setting a checkmark in the **View this collection in the Endpoint Protection dashboard** will make it show up here in **Monitoring | Overview | Security | Endpoint Protection Status**:

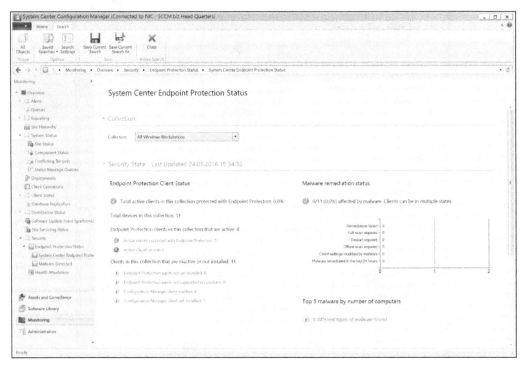

Endpoint Protection Status view in the Configuration Manager Console

Now, when you click on **Add** on the **Alerts** pane on the **Properties** of the collection you get the following page up, allowing you to enable what kind of alerts you want to have available on the specific collection:

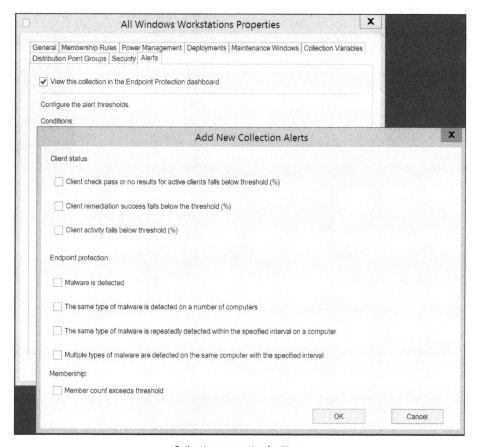

Collection properties for Alerts

4. I chose to select all just to show you all the available settings.

   I don't select the **Member count exceeds threshold** as it's not relevant in this case. It may be useful if you want to be alerted if the collection's members exceed a certain amount, or for monitoring computers with specific software, errors or similar.

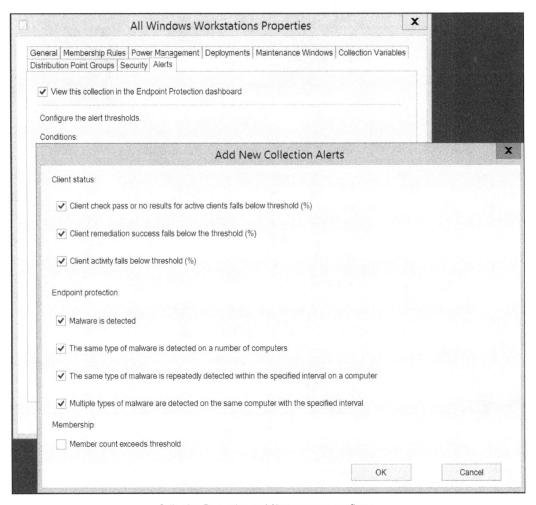

Collection Properties and Alerts you can configure.

5. On the next screen you will see different **Conditions** that you can set alerts on.

   Client check is important: This is the health check for the Configuration Manager client that is crucial for the Endpoint Protection client to get policies and forwards alerts about detected malware among other functions.

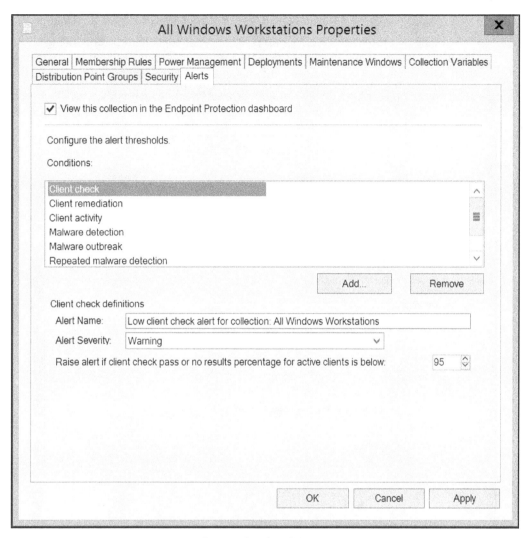

Alerts settings for a Collection

Another setting that I consider important is **Malware detection**.

You can view all malware that is detected in the Configuration Manager console, but you can choose to have the logs sent out by email so that many people in the IT department can easily view them and see what's going on without needing access to the console. One way to achieve this is to set the detection level to **High – All detections** as shown in the following screenshot.

Then, regardless of the detection and action, Endpoint Protection will alert via email.

The setting that is more suitable for an IT Manager or Administrator, depending on the size of the company, might be to set the Detection Level to Medium or Low to only alert when malware is not removed automatically and a manual action is required.

You can see more details on the different levels of alerting on the Microsoft Technet page: `https://technet.microsoft.com/en-us/library/hh508782.aspx`

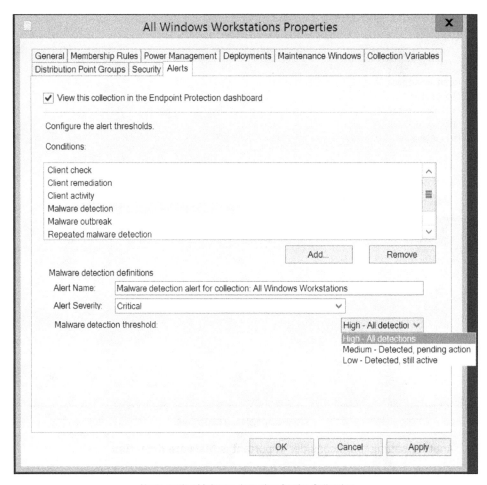

Alerts setting Malware detection for the Collection

6. A malware outbreak is definitely something that you would want to know about as well. Set the appropriate percentage of computers as shown in following screenshot.

7. Be aware that 5% might be a high number if you have 250.000 clients in that Collection.

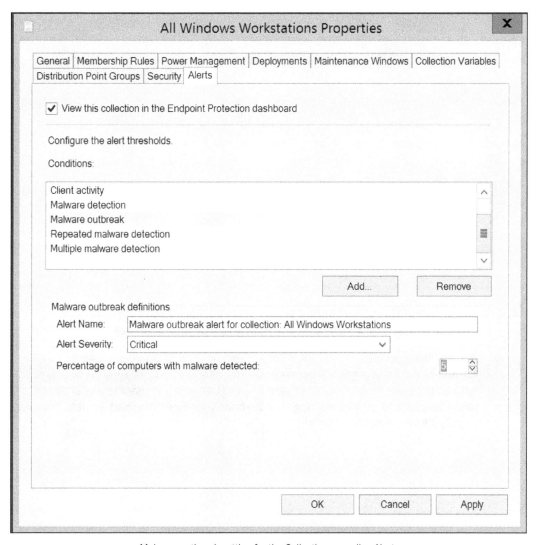

Malware outbreak setting for the Collection regarding Alerts

8. When you are finished setting the appropriate alert thresholds, the next phase is email configuration and subscriptions.

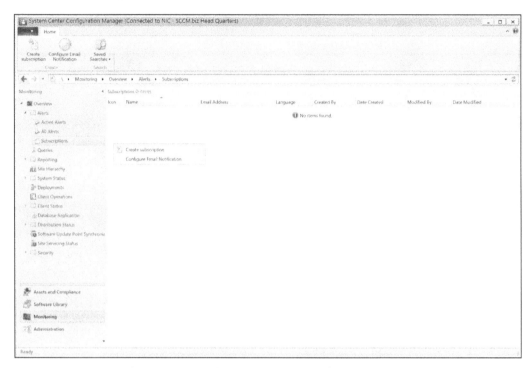

Configuration Manager Console you can create a Subscription for alerts

9. The first thing you need to set up, if you haven't already, is **Configure Email Notification**. This is a general configuration for all alerts in Configuration Manager, not just Endpoint Protection. You might need to talk to the IT team responsible for email solutions to get this working, and perhaps your Firewall expert as well. However, usually it's very easy to configure.

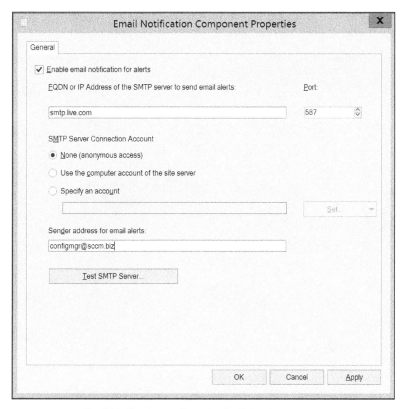

Email Notification configuration for Subscription Alerts.

10. Next, click **Create a new subscription**.

Enter the address you want to receive the alerts and select the **Alert** you want for that recipient.

The three that I mentioned earlier are the ones I find important to at least consider being alerted about. They are shown in the following screenshot:

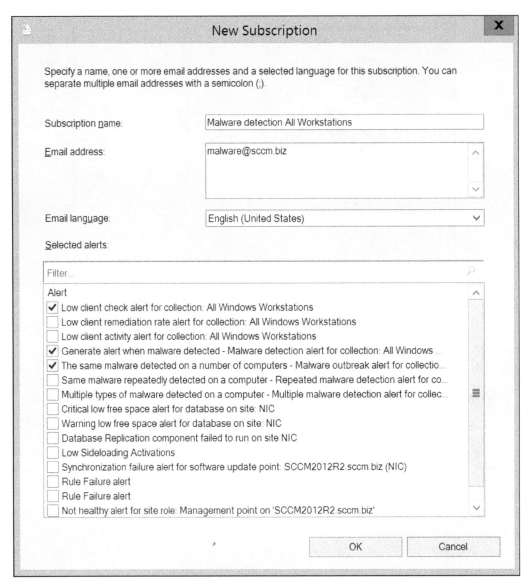

Alert Subscription for Malware detection of a Collection

How it works...

So, the Endpoint Protection client detects malware, then the Configuration Manager client fetches this and forwards it to it the site server and the site server forwards the email to the defined subscription based on the Alert level.

As you can see, you can have different subscriptions for different subscribers. You may differentiate subscriptions based on location or who has responsibility for that client(s). This will ensure the right people are informed as quickly as possible.

Configuring definition updates for Endpoint Protection in Configuration Manager

With Endpoint Protection in Microsoft System Center Configuration Manager, there are several available methods to deploy and update antimalware definitions as well as engine updates to the clients in your hierarchy.

Microsoft has its own antimalware signatures just like other competitive products on the market. Keeping the engine and client up-to-date is also very important as this is constantly improved with new features and more advanced detection methods. An example of this is the KB update: `https://support.microsoft.com/en-gb/kb/2998627`.

This will upgrade the Endpoint Protection client with an improved scanning ability and different optimizations regarding finding viruses better, rootkits, as well as malware.

We will show you how to keep both definitions and the client up-to-date.

Getting ready

To achieve this, you need to have System Center Configuration Manager setup, configured and running. And you need both the Software Update role and the Endpoint Protection role setup and configured.

Then you will be ready to configure the definition updates for Endpoint Protection.

How to do it...

There are several methods to get the Endpoint Protection client updated and these are:

- ▶ From Configuration Manager
- ▶ From WSUS
- ▶ From a Microsoft update

> ▸ From the Microsoft Malware Protection Center
>
> ▸ From the **Universal Naming Convention** (**UNC**) file share

You can use all of these methods in a specific order if you like, I would recommend this because they will work as a failsafe mechanism: if something were to happen with the first update source, it will go to the next source after a given time. You can adjust the time lapse between sources.

The update option I rarely use is the UNC file share, but it has been helpful in cases where some clients had issues with getting a Windows update to work, or had a similar problem.

I recommend you follow the order mentioned preceding and that the primary and first update source is via the Configuration Manager. This is very efficient and cost effective when considering bandwidth use throughout your hierarchy. The definition updates would only travel once, compressed from the primary site to your distribution points.

The update source order and configuration are done in the Endpoint Protection policy.

In the next chapter we will go into more detail on policies and how to monitor Endpoint Protection. For now, this is where you will find and configure the the update source order and where you will find the **Default Client Antimalware Policy**:

Create and configure Endpoint Protection Policies in the Configuration Manager Console

Be aware of the Policy order. The **Default Client Antimalware Policy** has as very low order **10000**. So, when you create more policies they will override the **Default** settings. But you need to have an understanding of this and keep the order correct when you have several policies deployed to same Collection.

In the **Definition updates** section you will find the default settings which you can adjust as you find appropriate for your corporate situation.

Be aware that the changes you make in the default policy will be effective for all the clients that have Endpoint Protection installed and enabled in this Configuration Manager site. I recommend that you create your own Endpoint Protection policy and make adjustments individually from there, unless you are absolutely sure that these settings should be set as default for everyone.

The Update Source order that you see on the following two screenshots, where the button is named **Set Source**, can be such a setting. It should be defined by the Configuration Manager Architect or administrator who knows how and what is best suited for your hierarchy and network.

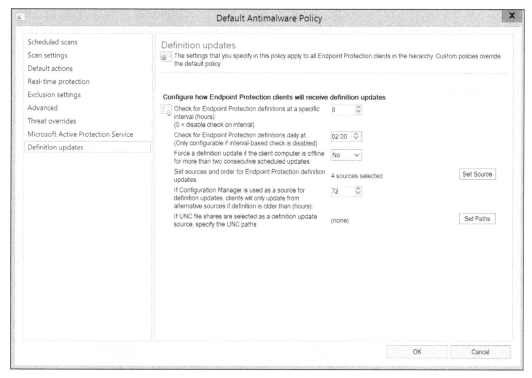

Definition Updates configuration settings within a Endpoint Protection Policy

I usually define a lower value for the frequency or interval of time at which clients should be set to check for definition updates. Perhaps two or four hours, depending on the amount of clients and network topology.

However, Microsoft delivers new definitions at most three times a day.

I would also consider changing the jump to alternative source from the default **72** hours, as you can see on the preceding screenshot, to 24 or 48 hours.

The default settings here are set to preserve your network infrastructure from saturation caused by high download activity, and so that you will be able to detect any misconfiguration and do repairs if necessary.

When you click the **Set Source** button on the right, you will see the default order of Update Sources that you can adjust up and down depending on the priority you want.

In this case, if the client cannot reach Configuration Manager or something is wrong with that update source, it will jump to the next source after the gap of hours you set. The default is **72** hours.

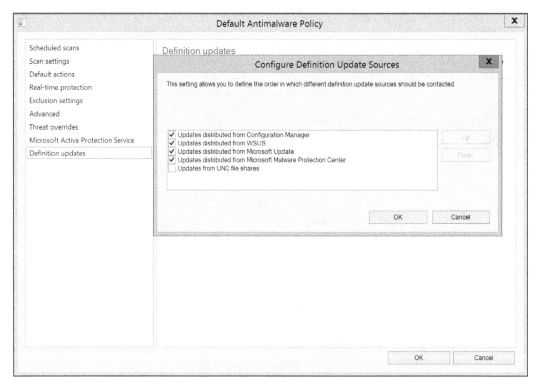

Definition Update Source order that you can configure in the Endpoint Protection Policy

How it works...

As I said in the first chapter of this book, Microsoft is good at using existing technology. So the built-in Windows Update component in Windows is used to download definition updates for Endpoint Protection using the **Background Intelligent Transfer Service** (**BITS**). The client then fetches and applies these.

However, Endpoint Protection also has a feature enabling it to fetch the definitions using the UNC file share. **Distributed File Shares** (**DFS**) would be suitable for keeping this UNC file share up-to-date.

See also

You can find more information about the UNC file shares, at the following address, where you will also find a PowerShell script that can keep it up-to-date with the latest definitions:

```
https://technet.microsoft.com/en-us/library/gg398041.aspx
```

Provisioning the Endpoint Protection client in a disk image in Configuration Manager

The Endpoint Protection client can be pre-installed on a computer that you want to use as a reference computer for the Configuration Manager operating system deployment. You can then deploy this disk image which also contains software packages, including Endpoint Protection client to your client computers or for setting up new computers.

What purpose or benefit could there be in provisioning the Endpoint Protection client in the disk image?

It will save some time during massive operating system deployments. On the other hand, on a daily basis you will need to maintain and update your Disk Image more often to ensure you have the latest Endpoint Protection client.

Getting ready

You need to have SCCM with the Software Update role and the Endpoint Protection role setup and fully configured.

You need access to the `scepinstall.exe` that can be found in the `Configuration Manager Client` folder.

Ensure that the Endpoint Protection client is deployed in your organization using the required settings and configuration. You need to specify an antimalware policy when you install Endpoint Protection clients manually. For this, you have to export the policy, and this policy cannot be the default Endpoint Protection policy.

How to do it...

Either you use the **Build** and **Capture Task Sequence** or you do it manually. You need to make a package of the `scepinstall.exe` with the policy file.

You can export the policy from within the **Configuration Manager** console:

All Workstations Custom Policy created in the Endpoint Protection Policy

You export the manually defined policy to XML and add it to the folder with the `scepinstall.exe` file.

The installation command is:

```
scepinstall.exe /policy polcyfilename.xml
```

If you use the **Build** and **Capture Task Sequence** that I recommend using when building Disk Images, you need to create a software package with the two files and run it as a command or program during the **Task** Sequence.

More information about provisioning an Endpoint Protection client in a Disk Image in Configuration Manager is available from:

```
https://technet.microsoft.com/en-us/library/dn236350.aspx.
```

3
Operations and Maintenance for Endpoint Protection in Configuration Manager

In this chapter, we will cover the following recipes:

- ▶ Creating and deploying antimalware policies for Endpoint Protection in Configuration Manager
- ▶ Creating and deploying Windows Firewall policies for Endpoint Protection in Configuration Manager
- ▶ Monitoring Endpoint Protection in Configuration Manager

Introduction

In this chapter, we will demonstrate the combined strength and flexibility of Endpoint Protection and Configuration Manager. You can target any system you want, as long as it has the client software installed with whatever policy configuration you would like. Configuration Manager will ensure that it is enforced and applied to the targeted system. But surely you can do this somewhat with other antimalware products as well, so why is this different? Because with Configuration Manager, you also have a full inventory of both hardware and software on every server and workstation, and you have integration to Active Directory as well.

All this information is put together and at your disposal in a database. This means you can target whatever you want and have it update automatically if this would make it easier to maintain. One of the huge benefits of running System Center Endpoint Protection regarding this is that it contains out-of-the-box policy for many known products such as Domain Controller, Exchange, SQL, Terminal Servers, and so on, with exclusions settings in place. All you need to do is import them, check that the folder path is correct regarding your installation, and perhaps make any final changes before deploying it to dedicated collections. It's as easy as that.

Creating and deploying antimalware policies for Endpoint Protection in Configuration Manager

Antimalware policies are easy to deploy to collections of Configuration Manager Clients and will specify how Endpoint Protection protects them from different malware and threats. Several settings, such as the scan schedule, the types of files and folders to scan, and actions taken when malware is detected are typical settings that you would configure in the policies to fit the targeted computers.

When you enable Endpoint Protection on your client computers, the default Endpoint Protection policy is applied. You may also use additional policy templates, which you can import from the console, or create your own custom policies to meet the specific needs of your environment.

How to do it...

This is how your default antimalware policy in Endpoint Protection looks and will be applied to all your Configuration Manager clients that have the Endpoint Protection client installed and enabled.

I recommend that you don't make changes to this policy other than the definition updates shown in the following screenshot:

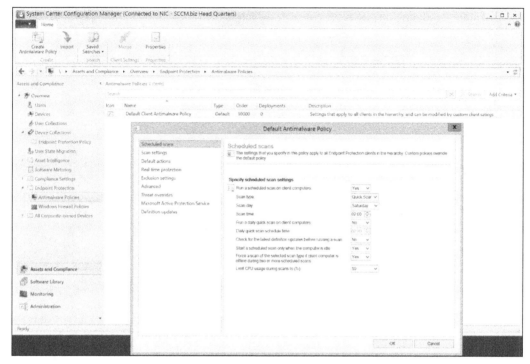

Default Antimalware Policy

You can see the **Definition updates** settings, in the **Default Antimalware Policy**, in the following screenshot.

I would recommend that you define in the **Default Antimalware Policy** what **Update Sources** order and configure settings that would suite most of your Endpoint Protection clients. That way, if the computer should not receive any other Custom defined policy for whatever reason, it will at least get definitions updates correctly, which is the most essential thing for it to work properly:

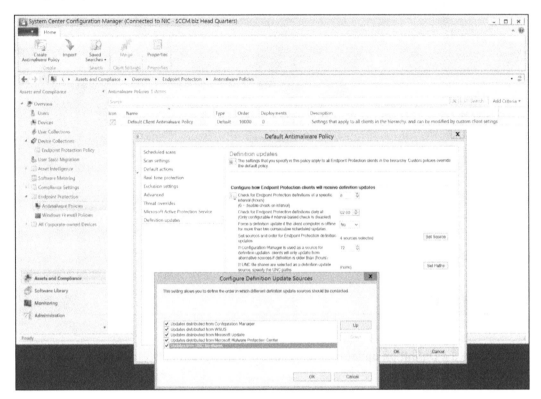

Update Sources order in the Default Antimalware Policy

The order shown in the preceding screenshot is the default order, and I've checked the updates from the **Universal Naming Convention** (**UNC**) file share as well. As described in *Chapter 2, Configuring Endpoint Protection in Configuration Manager* about Definition updates, you need to think this through and plan according to how Configuration Manager is installed, how its hierarchy is defined, and what your network looks like.

The default order is the recommended one, and I wouldn't change it if you don't have any special requirements. But you need to know that the clients won't be able to fetch any definition updates from WSUS if you have not entered the WSUS Console and set up **Automatic Definition** rule there. You should not make any other changes in the WSUS console.

However, you need to think this through. If you have 20,000 clients in an office located on the other side of the world communicating over a 2 Mb network link connection, you might not want them to fetch definition updates from the WSUS Server at your primary site headquarters just because something is wrong with the Configuration Manager distribution points.

I would also recommend keeping the last two options selected as well. These are the updates from Microsoft Malware Protection Center and UNC file shares, and they will kick in as a failsafe method for the Endpoint Protection clients to fetch the definitions updates if the Windows updates or Configuration Manage client should somehow cease to work or fail.

Keeping this order and all settings correct should ensure that all your clients should work as safely as possible.

Other antimalware that I've worked with doesn't have a good monitoring solution to detect if a client fails to respond and no longer applies updates. A worse case scenario would be to find out which machines do not have anti-malware product installed and why do they not have it.

Order and combination of policies to be merged

It's important to know that if you have several policies deployed to the same targeted systems with the same specified settings, only the specified setting from policy with highest precedence will be applied, depending on the order.

Meaning policies do merge with precedence order in consideration. So, you can actually approach this in many ways depending on what suites your needs in the best way. Also, the fact that this works dynamically with constantly updated collections makes this highly unique compared to other similar products.

You can in fact have several policies like DNS, DHCP and Active Directory deployed to each collection and have several servers automatically queried based on what software application they have installed.

There is also another merge feature that will allow you to create a new custom policy based on the settings from two or more policies. Let's say you have DNS and DHCP roles on your domain controllers, which is very common in small- to medium-sized companies, you would want to import those three policies and merge them. This is done by selecting the policies and then selecting **Merge** from the menu:

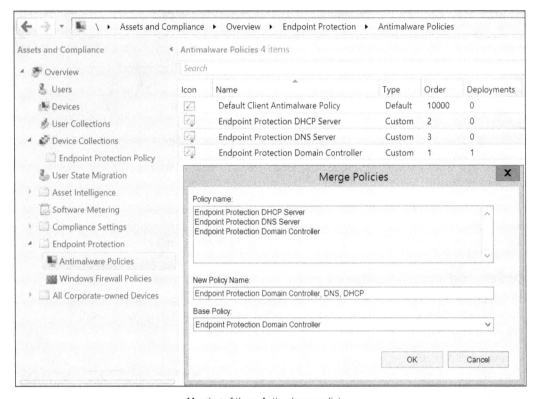

Merging of three Antimalware policies.

You would then want to deploy the policy created to a collection containing all the Active Directory Domain Controller servers in your domain.

You could create a query on the collection like this to query the **Organization Unit** (**OU**), as shown in the following screenshot:

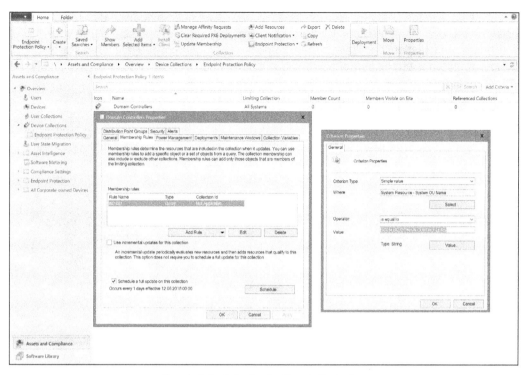

Querying of a Collection for Domain Controllers

For example, we have an **Endpoint Protection Policy** and we want to target all our Domain Controller servers with this policy. We also want all new Domain Controllers installed later to automatically get this policy as well. We can do this in different ways, but a quick and easy way to do it is to create a collection and query it to target systems that are in the Domain Controller Organization Unit within Active Directory and then target the policy to that OU. The collection will update itself hereafter based on the settings you apply. The default is every seven days, and if you want it updated as fast as possible, you check the incremental update option, which will kick in an update cycle every 10 minutes. Be aware, however, that this option should only be used on a maximum of 200 collections within the Configuration Manager hierarchy. A symptom that may easily occur if a larger number of collections is used is that the update fails, meaning that the content of the collections is not correct and may show as empty, or with a lack of consistency. I've seen this occur where there were around 500 collections with this feature enabled.

But going back to the Endpoint Protection policy, why do we need a dedicated configured policy for our Domain Controllers, Exchange Servers, SQL Servers, and so on? This is a very important question, and is very often overlooked or forgotten. You might not see any obvious symptoms, errors, or faults, but it is recommended by Microsoft that you configure antimalware exclusion settings regardless of what antimalware system you might be running. This is to ensure that nothing will hold, delay, or compromise the application or system running on that server or workstation. For example, on Domain Controllers, it's important that the **System Volume** (**SYSVOL**) folder structure is excluded to ensure that domain function and replication are fully functional and work as quickly and smoothly as they should. Different behavior may occur depending on the antimalware product, but I have seen replication issues, as well as slow replication, on servers that are running with real-time scanning on these folders.

It is important to exclude any databases from antimalware real-time scanning. Otherwise, failure, or at least slow database performance and high CPU usage, will occur:

 Now Microsoft has a guideline for what folders and processes that should be excluded: `https://support.microsoft.com/en-us/kb/943556`.

Collection Criteria of the Domain Controllers in Active Directory

It may also be wise to decrease the **Schedule a full update on this collection** to every day:

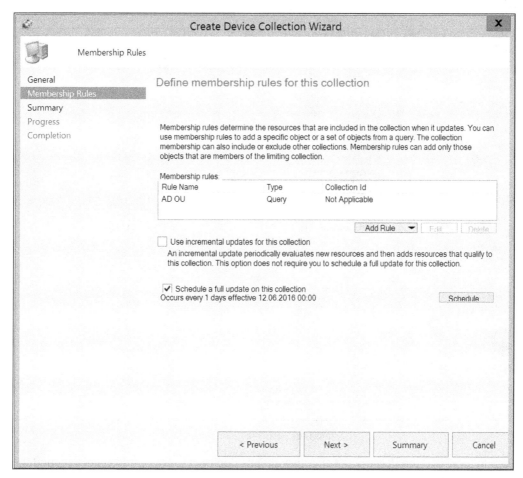

Collection update settings

After creating the collection, you will see the hourglass on the icon of the collection working for a few seconds while it's running the update. You can then hit the **Refresh** button and confirm that it contains what you want.

Then, you deploy the Endpoint Protection to that collection, and you're done, as shown in the following screenshot:

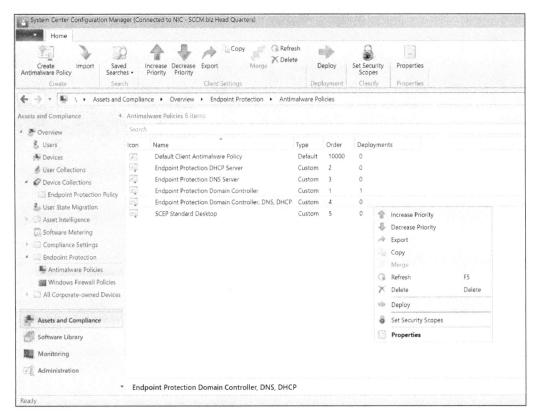

Antimalware policy ready deployment

Keep in mind that the Policy is not effective until its deployed to a targeted collection, and the computer or server has received the new policy. The Configuration Manager database usually needs a few seconds to process, as well. Now, this is one of the things that is essential to understand when working with Configuration Manager, that usually things needs a little bit a patience before it starts to work, because it's a large machinery and many parallel processes going on and they each have their schedule cycle to work with.

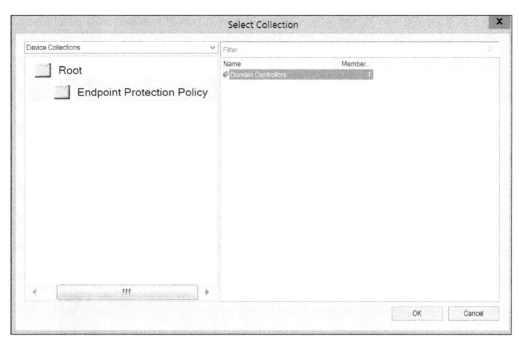

Collection choice you have when deploying the Policy

The settings will be applied to the clients on their next **Machine Policy Retrieval & Evaluation Cycle**. You can view the settings within the Endpoint Protection client GUI:

Actions you have available within the Configuration Manager Properties on the Client

Another way to make a collection is to make a query based on what application is installed on it. The following screenshot shows an example of a SQL 2012 Server query:

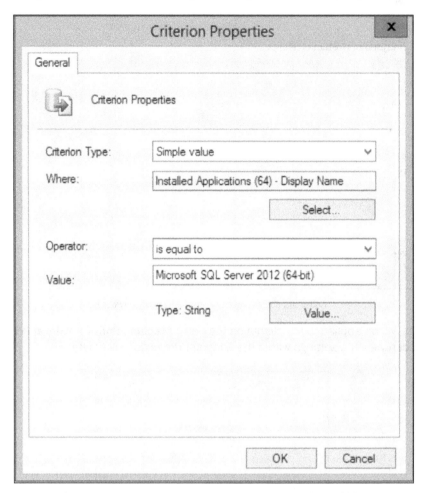

Collection query for Installed Applications Microsoft SQL Server 2012

Collections based on a query will automatically update themselves with new members as more systems with Configuration Manager clients are installed and inventoried.

You could, of course, just create a plain collection with no queries and add systems manually by right-clicking the collection and choosing **Add Resources**. That would be the easiest and quickest way, but requires a little maintenance. However, I would recommend that you do a little bit of work getting the queries right from the start as a good practice, this will ensure that every server, service or application will have its proper policy to work properly.

Exclusions

In the *Introduction* to this chapter, you read about the importance of exclusions, especially when it comes to servers, and applications running on servers, such as Active Directory, SQL, Exchange, and so on.

One of the advantages of Endpoint Protection is that it contains several ready-made policies from Microsoft, as shown in the following screenshot:

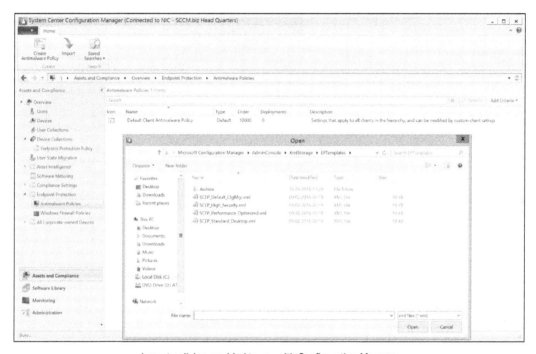

Import policies provided to you with Configuration Manager

When you click on **Import** while that you on the **Antimalware Policies** screen, you can import those xml files that are policies with settings defined by Microsoft best practice.

In the `Archive` folder, you will find more policies, as shown in the following screenshot:

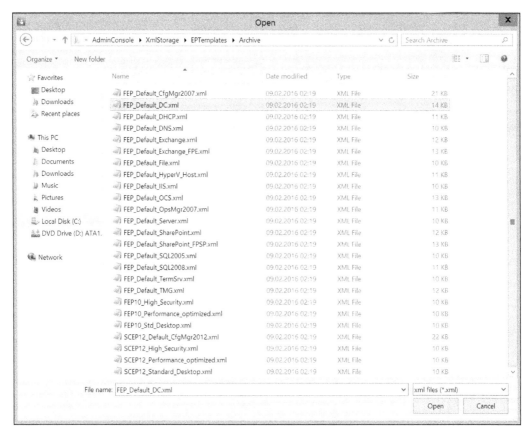

Several policies for the different Windows Server Roles or Applications.

For System Center Operation Manager 2007 and newer, you need to use the `FEP_Default_OpsMgr2007.xml` policy

For Window Server File Services, you need to use the `FEP_Default_File.xml` policy.

After importing your chosen policy, you can view the settings. You may find the essential settings in the exclusion section. There might be some settings on file system behavior for File Servers, and so on:

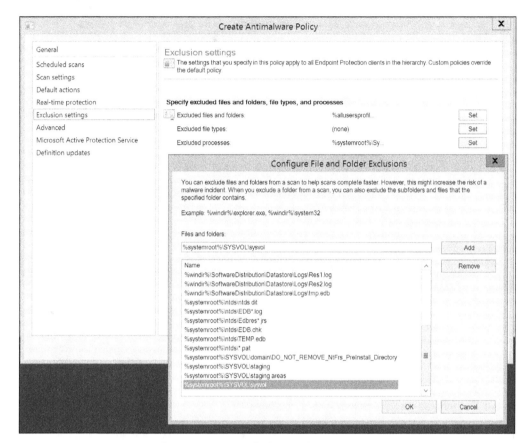

Exclusions the policy for Domain Controllers have

The preceding screenshot shows that the SYSVOL folder is excluded in the DC policy.

Process exclusions are shown in the following screenshot:

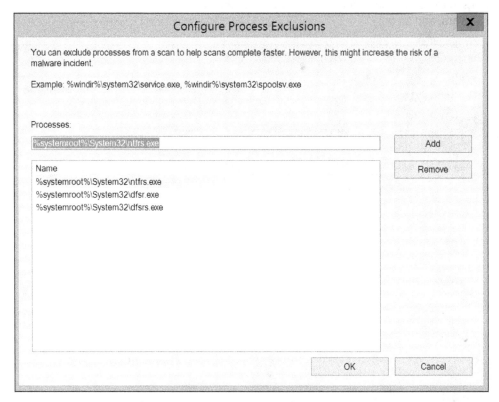

Processes excluded in the Domain Controllers policy

You will find similar exclusions in the other policies.

After updating your Configuration Manager Site to version 1602, you will get an improved Endpoint Protection that enables, by default, a new feature called **Potentially Unwanted Applications**.

This will perform a real-time scan on all `.exe` files that might have been modified and added such as toolbar, ad-ware, dialer, password stealers, and so on. This is a very new feature that will definitely have uses in every corporation.

The following screenshot shows you the default real-time protection. From version 1602 onward, you have the new Potential Unwanted Applications feature.

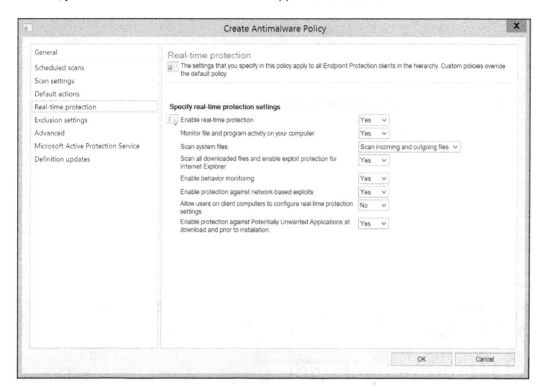

The following screenshot shows an example of what you might find being detected and quarantined:

Malware detected in a production environment

Creating and deploying Windows Firewall policies for Endpoint Protection in Configuration Manager

When it comes to Firewall, System Center Endpoint Protection has no built-in firewall of its own; it mostly relies on Windows Firewall doing the job. Now, you might think the Windows Firewall is not good enough to protect your computers. With Windows XP, and even Windows 7, it is true that the firewall was maybe not top-notch and had room for improvement, but when Microsoft released the new platform Windows 8, and from there on up, it was a whole new matter. These systems included a brand-new Firewall with more advanced features, which has just kept improving as it has evolved.

That said, System Center Endpoint Protection has its own built-in features, like most of its competitors, for detecting and protecting against network exploits and massive attacks. This is important, as I often see customers running their Windows Server and workstations with the Windows Firewall switched OFF while in the Domain profile, and only switched ON with the Public Networks profile. Now, it's highly recommended by Microsoft and security specialists to have your Windows Firewall turned ON at all times on both workstations and servers, no matter how many firewalls you might have between your internal network and the Internet. Having it turned on will give you monitoring as well, and logging that might be useful so that you can pick up and detect network traffic on your servers that shouldn't actually be there. Using System Center Operation Manager or the cloud product, Operation Management Suite, as an example, you will be able to pick up that kind of information pretty easily if you're running with your Windows Firewall switched ON.

You can, of course, run another Firewall product on your workstations if you like. Just make the appropriate rule exception for System Center Configuration Manager Client and any other applications and management tools you might have.

Let's have a closer look at what we can do.

How to do it...

Group Policy Forcing Firewall settings are most commonly used as compared to OU or Security Groups. That is a simple and force full solution to make the Firewall configuration. Since 2012, you now have the ability to deploy this as a configuration as well. But why use this feature in System Center Configuration Manager?

Well, for one, it will give you the benefit of monitoring the results and more deployment flexibility within your organization. This means that you can deploy this Firewall configuration to any kind of targeted machine, as long as it has the Configuration Manager client installed and running. As mentioned earlier, Collections are based on many kinds of criteria such as, domains, computer model information, kind of role, IP subnet, naming, installed application information just to name a few. You might also catch some machines that someone has moved out of the OU where you specified the Group Policy that configures the Windows Firewall. Therefore, I would say that it is best to use both Group Policy and the Windows Firewall policy with System Center. But remember, Group Policy wins.

You might have Workgroup Clients or Servers in DMZ where this feature would be very handy to configure Windows Firewall via SCCM.

The basic tasks you can configure are as follows:

▶ Either **Enable** or **Disable** Windows Firewall within the different profiles

▶ Block incoming traffic, as well including those in the list of allowed programs

▶ Choose whether or not to notify the user when Windows Firewall blocks a new program

In the following screenshot, you can see the creation of a Windows Firewall Policy, and what configuration you can define, in the System Center Configuration Manager console:

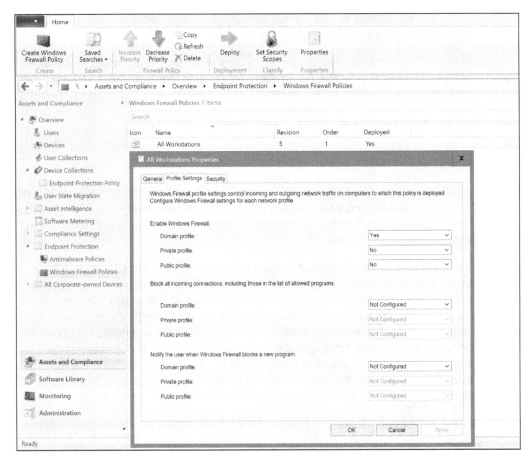

Settings for creating a Firewall Policy

So, how this works is like this:

If you don't have a Group Policy that defines the Windows Firewall settings, the Endpoint Protection Windows Firewall Policy will be effective.

If you have a Group Policy as well as an Endpoint Protection Windows Firewall policy, then you can think of the policy shown in the preceding screenshot as a compliance baseline, where you will get a report back on what status the computers have regarding the settings you define.

You can find the Group Policy setting for this in `Computer Configuration\Policies\ Administrative Templates..\Network\Network Connections\Windows Firewall\`.

This is shown in the following screenshot:

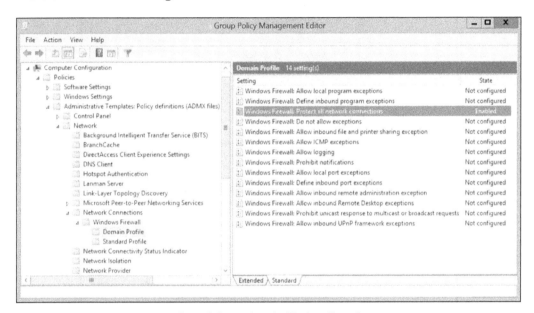

Group Policy settings for Windows Firewall

You can also use the **Advanced Security** settings that were released from Windows 2008 and Vista. This will give you a more granular control and give you the ability to control both inbound and outbound communication.

The settings are found in **Windows Settings | Security Settings | Windows Firewall with Advanced Security**:

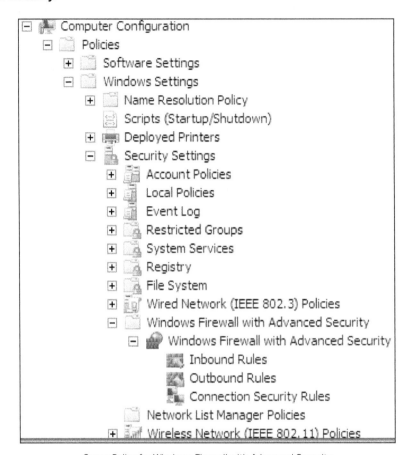

Group Policy for Windows Firewall with Advanced Security

After creating the Endpoint Protection Windows Firewall policy, deploying it to a collection of computers is a very common procedure in System Center Configuration Manager:

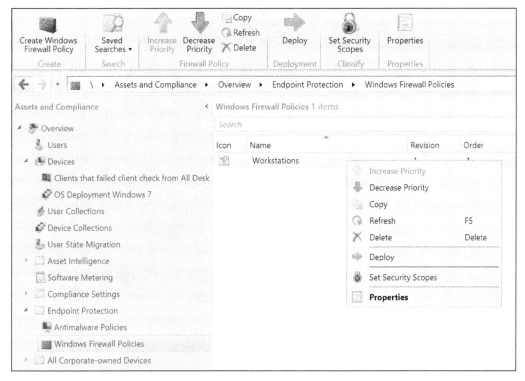

Workstations policy we created and the options present

The following screenshot shows the **Deploy Windows Firewall Policy** window, where you define how often the compliance baseline will be evaluated:

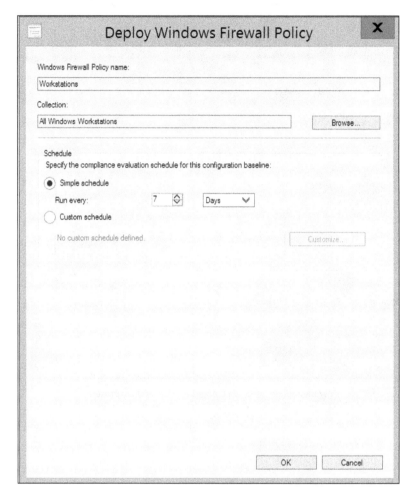

Default Simple schedule of the Compliance evaluation of the baseline

If we head on over to a computer that will receive this policy and perform a Machine Policy update on the Configuration Manager client, you can see that the policy has arrived as a configuration baseline. You can trigger the evaluation manually.

The following screenshot shows you the actions you have in the Configuration Manager application from the **Control Panel** in Windows:

The following screenshot shows you that baselines are received in the Configuration Manager client, and that it is evaluated as **Compliant**:

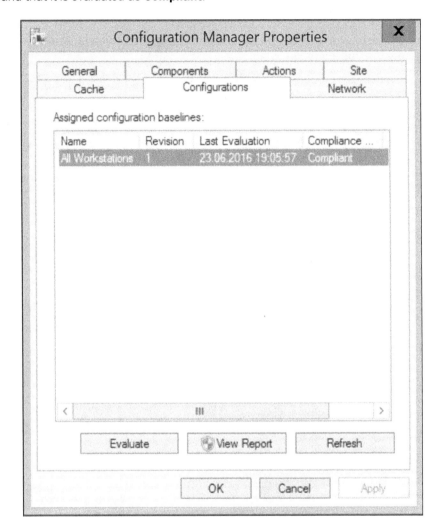

If you are local administrator, you get to see a report as well:

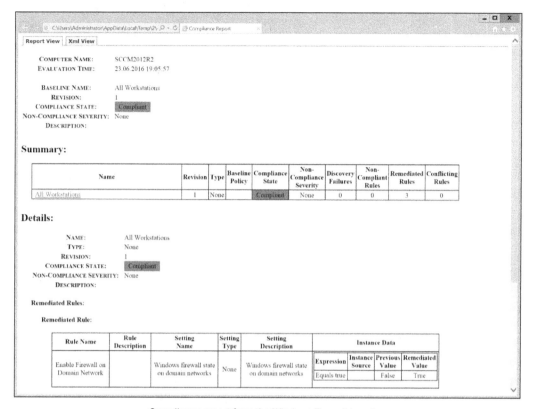

Compliance report from the Windows Firewall baseline

The Windows Firewall in Windows will show you a message that some settings are managed by your system administrator if you have either a Group Policy or Endpoint Protection Windows Firewall policy, as shown in the following screenshot:

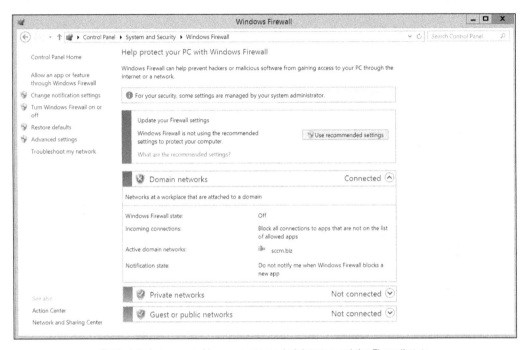

Settings being managed by your system administrator and the Firewall state

To monitor the compliance level and get more details on how the policy compliance is heading in your environment, you can go to the **Monitoring | Overview | Deployments** page and choose to view the rule you deployed. Remember that it may take a while until you get results back on this one, depending on your settings. Then you have to hit **Run Summarization and Refresh** to get an update in the view.

When you click on a **Compliant** listed, you will get more details on the status of the compliance as you can see on the picture following:

Deployment status in the Configuration Manager Console of the Windows Firewall setting that are deployed to the clients.

Monitoring Endpoint Protection in Configuration Manager

Monitoring Endpoint Protection is a very nice and important feature. There are several ways to monitor it in your System Center Configuration Manager hierarchy. Specifically in the Monitoring workspace, the Endpoint Protection node in the Assets and Compliance workspace, and by using reports.

Another very nice product that is supporting SCCM more and more is Power BI. This is an advanced website that can be configured to present important information such as antimalware, software updates, deployment and client health information, live.

The following link will give you more information:

`https://powerbi.microsoft.com/en-us/solution-templates/sccm/`

How to do it...

Be aware that when the Windows 10 Health Attestation feature is Enabled during installation of Configuration Manager 1602 update or later, the **Endpoint Protection Status** is moved permanently to a folder called `Security`, as shown in the following screenshot:

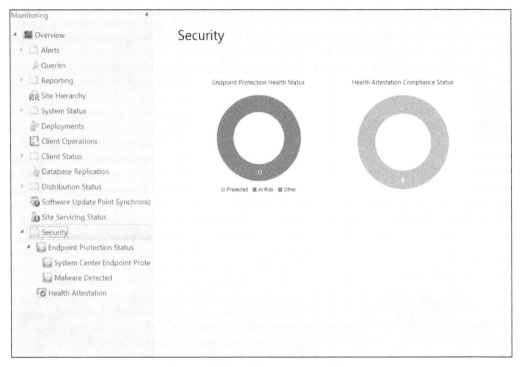

Windows 10 Health Attestation is enabled

The Windows 10 Health Attestation feature is also permanently installed and cannot be removed:

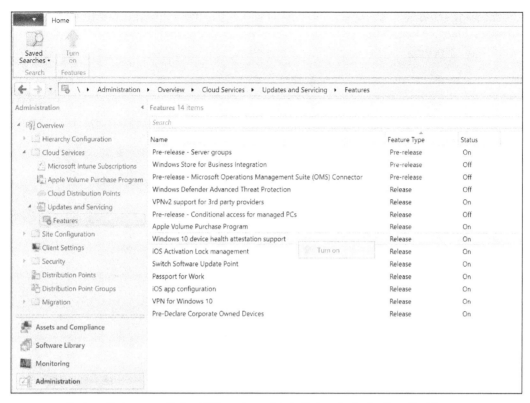

Features that comes with the 1602 version update in System Center Configuration Manager

If you don't have that feature added, it will look like that shown in the following screenshot.

Without the `Security` folder in the console menu, notice that you can choose the collection you want to view the status of.

These collections either have an Endpoint Protection policy, or have enabled this in the **Alerts** tab on the collection properties.

This will also adjust itself, as Configuration Manager administrator might have different rights to their respective collections for their organization or unit. This is so that you can only view information on the clients you are responsible for.

The following screenshot shows you the default settings, without the Windows 10 Health Attestation feature installed:

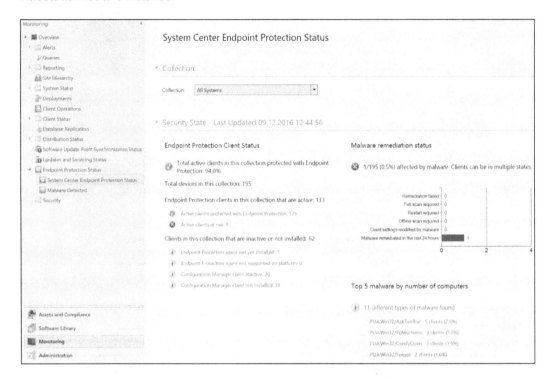

The following screenshot shows a list of malware found in the different collections.

You can click on **View Clients** to get more information about which computers have detected this malware. You can also view which files have been modified.

The following figure shows you the typical malware you might find on computers within the different collections:

You will also find a number of reports providing useful information and some history graphs. I found the history graphs especially useful when dealing with a massive malware outbreak spreading among thousands of computers. I could then see, from hour to hour and day by day, that the actions we were taking were helping, as the graphs provided very useful information about the progress.

If you only get fresh, real-time data, it's not so easy to see if this is going in the right direction in the bigger picture. For that, you need statistics.

The following screenshot shows the folder where you will find the Endpoint Protection reports:

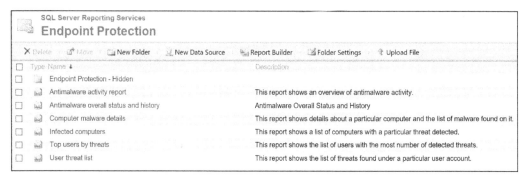

	Type	Name ↓	Description
☐		Endpoint Protection - Hidden	
☐		Antimalware activity report	This report shows an overview of antimalware activity.
☐		Antimalware overall status and history	Antimalware Overall Status and History
☐		Computer malware details	This report shows details about a particular computer and the list of malware found on it.
☐		Infected computers	This report shows a list of computers with a particular threat detected.
☐		Top users by threats	This report shows the list of users with the most number of detected threats.
☐		User threat list	This report shows the list of threats found under a particular user account.

SQL Reporting Services Web page for System Center Configuration Manager – Endpoint Protection folder

The following screenshot shows you an example from a production environment where malware was detected over a period of time.

You may find some of the reports interesting.

There are also reports that will show you what the top-rated domain users , list of malware incidents, and also the top-rated computers as shown in the picture following:

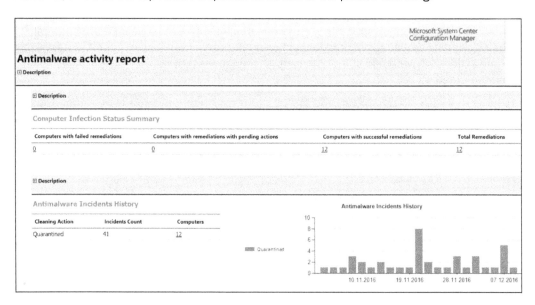

The following screenshot shows you what malware has been detected and when, and how many computers are affected:

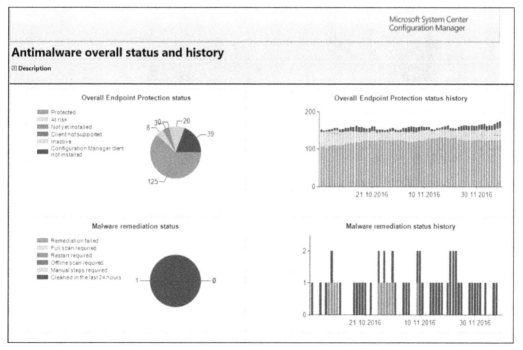

Microsoft System Center
Configuration Manager

Top malware by severity
⊞ Description

Top Malware By Severity						All
Threat Name	Category	Severity	Computers	Incidents Count	First Detection (UTC)	Latest Detection (UTC)
PUA:Win32/AskToolbar	Potentially Unwanted Software	Severe	5	6	21.11.2016 05:21:16	30.11.2016 12:44:49
PUA:Win32/CandyOpen	Potentially Unwanted Software	Severe	3	4	08.11.2016 15:22:19	22.11.2016 19:43:29
PUA:Win32/PcMechanic	Potentially Unwanted Software	Severe	3	3	21.11.2016 06:15:38	28.11.2016 08:04:00
PUA:Win32/Spigot	Potentially Unwanted Software	Severe	2	2	21.11.2016 09:29:22	21.11.2016 22:02:48
Trojan:Win32/Rundas!plock	Trojan	Severe	1	1	15.11.2016 08:36:47	15.11.2016 08:36:47
Trojan:Win32/Suweezy	Trojan	Severe	1	1	10.11.2016 07:48:10	10.11.2016 07:48:10
TrojanDownloader:JS/NeutrinoEK.Y	Trojan Downloader	Severe	1	3	07.12.2016 07:43:03	07.12.2016 07:44:12
VirTool:SWF/Injector.D	Tool	Severe	1	1	07.12.2016 07:43:30	07.12.2016 07:43:30
PUA:Win32/Pokavampo	Potentially Unwanted Software	Severe	1	1	09.11.2016 15:41:22	09.11.2016 15:41:22
PUA:Win32/SpeedChecker	Potentially Unwanted Software	Severe	1	1	09.11.2016 15:40:51	09.11.2016 15:40:51
PUA:Win32/InstallCore	Potentially Unwanted Software	Severe	1	18	04.11.2016 08:08:05	08.12.2016 13:41:07

This is the statistic chart report that I used often to view as an ongoing malware attack was spread among the clients. I specifically viewed the **Malware remediation status** history window. This was very red in color for a few days, but improved as more and more clients were remediated and protected:

Antimalware overall status and history over a given period of time

4

Updates

In this chapter, we will cover the following recipes:

- ▶ Understanding Endpoint Protection updates
- ▶ Working with updates from WSUS
- ▶ Working with updates from SCCM
- ▶ What you need to consider and optimize when working with low bandwidth locations
- ▶ Why and how to use offline updates

Introduction

It's obvious that having a good working solution for delivering definitions, engine updates as well as program updates is of the essence for security reasons. For example, it is important to have **Definition** updates to make **Endpoint Protection** able to detect new sorts of malwares and **Engine** updates, to improve Endpoint Protection with new methods and smart features.

But what do I mean by program updates? Well by this I mean that you have to keep up with new releases of the **System Center Configuration Manager** (**SCCM**). When you do an upgrade of SCCM you will get a new version of the SCCM client as well as the Endpoint Protection client agent.

In fact, when running the new platform from 1511, you must update your complete SCCM infrastructure to be at a supported level. Meaning, for example that support for SCCM version 1511 expires December 2016, that is twelve months after release date.

When you start the SCCM Console you will receive an alert if there are available updates for your site server like this:

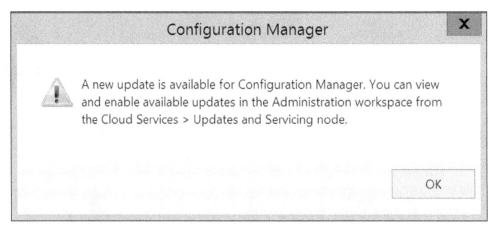

Configuration Manager　　　　X

A new update is available for Configuration Manager. You can view and enable available updates in the Administration workspace from the Cloud Services > Updates and Servicing node.

OK

Alert message when a new update is available for the SCCM site server.

Microsoft plans to release updates a few times per year, and will, during the first three months, deliver security and **critical updates** for the current version. After that, until the end of the support expires, Microsoft will only deliver **security updates**.

There are even more rapid updates for SCCM released called **Technical Preview**, but remember to not run this in your production environment. They cannot be mixed, meaning you cannot run a Technical Preview update to a **non-Preview** production version. Also you cannot turn a Technical Preview solution into a non-Preview version. This is strictly for testing out new features in a demo lab environment.

Understanding Endpoint Protection updates

How do Endpoint Protection Updates work with SCCM? This is a bit more complex compared to other antimalware products: Endpoint Protection has many ways to fetch the updates with the use of different technologies involved; and there are time settings that determine what happens, and when. This has its pros and cons.

The pros are that it makes it more failsafe. Endpoint Protection will most likely manage to update itself even if some functions fail. Another pro is that you can configure it to suit your environment in the best way to ensure the least disturbance and interference to employees.

The con that I see is that, if you get too many choices that you don't need, you are more likely to overlook or misconfigure them. When troubleshooting why only some of my clients have been updated and some not, it may be hard to figure out because of all the settings and time schedules, as well as figuring out where the client update came from. This requires some logical and thorough investigation similar to other functions in SCCM.

How to do it...

First it's important to mention that setting up and configuring an Endpoint Protection role along with a **Software Update Point** role are essential for this to work.

Configuration Manager will provide updates through the Software Update channel. Delays can be caused by misconfiguration, or components not working, clients being offline, policy, **Automatic Deployment Rules** (**ADR**), WSUS sync, and so on.

If the definitions get older than 72 hours (by default), then the Endpoint Protection or **Defender** agent is allowed to seek its own definitions; and pull them according to the source order list.

The source order is a bit of a misnomer, since Endpoint Protection or Defender don't know how to *pull* from Configuration Manager as they are not really aware of **Distribution Points** and all that logic. Moreover, most customers don't use the WSUS console so the definition updates aren't approved in **Windows Server Update Services** (**WSUS**); therefore Endpoint Protection or Defender won't download from the WSUS server.

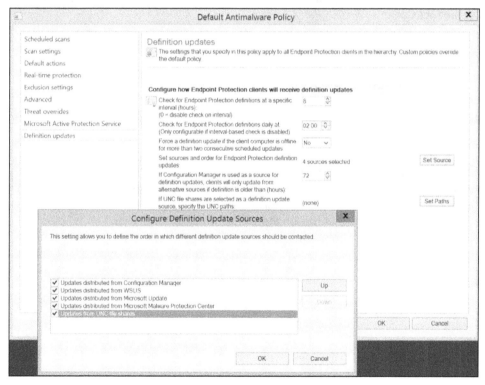

Definition Update Source order and settings

Working with updates from WSUS

How do updates from WSUS work, and when should we use them?

Getting ready

WSUS is an underlying **Prerequisite Service** that needs to be in place before you can set up and configure the SCCM role that is called **Software Updates**.

As mentioned earlier the Software Updates role will also do all the setup and configuration of the WSUS. That said, there are some further steps you need to take care of within the WSUS Console as well as the **Active Directory Group Policy Management Console**.

How to do it...

There has been, and still is, confusion around whether or not you need a Group Policy setting and Windows Update settings for the clients, since there are different opinions and experiences on this.

Why should I need a policy when the SCCM client is setting it for me? Wouldn't that be the easiest way to go?

Yes, the easiest, but not the safest way.

Well, as long as you have SCCM client agent installed and the **Software Update Point** (**SUP**) role working well, it's all good.

However, I would advise you to establish a **Group Policy** forcing the **Windows Update** settings for all your clients. By having this in place you have full control, and the clients are forced to that specific Software Update Point (WSUS) so that the Windows Update engine is able to update from the WSUS; or even more importantly so that all your clients do not download all available updates if for whatever reason there is no working SCCM client; or if the Software Update Point role is to be removed during troubleshooting for some reason. I have seen this happen: The Software Update Point role was uninstalled, and suddenly all the clients downloaded and installed the latest Internet Explorer. Not great fun, if your business it not yet ready for this.

A disadvantage of this scenario is that roaming clients traveling between different locations might not be utilize Windows Update scanning towards WSUS in the most efficient way at all times. However, this will most likely be a minor issue, and will result in slightly more network traffic between the locations.

This will of course depend on your SCCM hierarchy and structure, and might not be a topic to worry about at all if you have perhaps only one Software Update Point (WSUS) role in your hierarchy.

A client will still download updates from update packages from SCCM based on the **Boundary** settings you have. Another tip regarding Boundary settings: use the IP Range only to avoid the super netting issue. If you have several clients it will hit the SQL Database Server more and increase CPU usage.

Another aspect is that, if you are utilizing the SCCM client installation method, which pushes the client though WSUS to the client machines, wouldn't that be another reason to have a Group Policy defining your Software Update Point (WSUS)?

So this is the Group Policy setting you need to link to your SCCM clients **Organization Unit** (**OU**) in Active Directory.

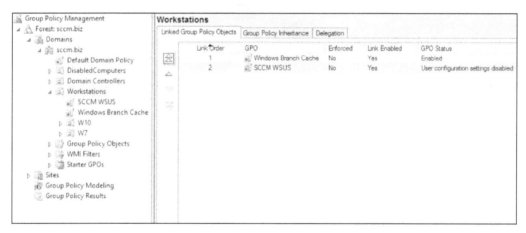

Group Policy Management

In the object I have created called **SCCM WSUS** I chose to disable **User configuration settings** because this speeds up the Group Policy processing as I have no need to configure any user-based policy settings regarding this.

When you open the policy object there are two settings that you have to define in `Policies\ Administrator Templates\Windows Components\Windows Update\:`

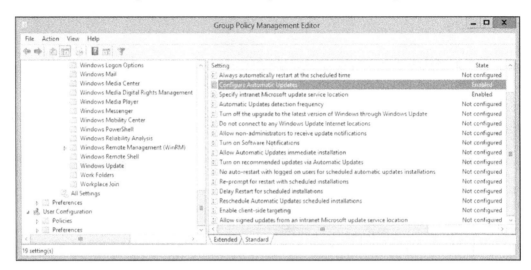

Different settings within Windows Update GPO

The following screenshot shows you the first setting you need to configure for **Automatic Updates**.

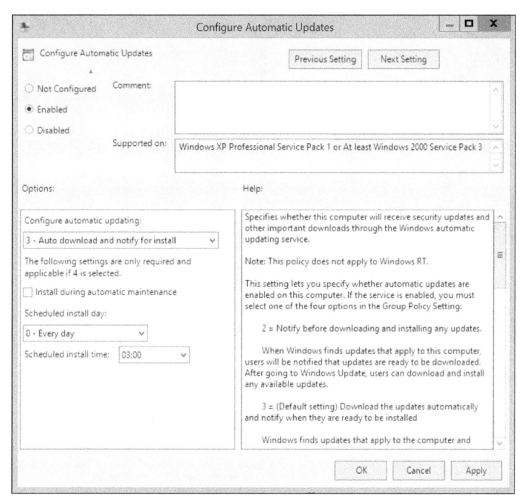

Configuring for Automatic Updates

You just need to **Enable** it and SCCM will do the rest.

Updates deployed through SCCM will have their own schedule setting working together with the SCCM client agent settings.

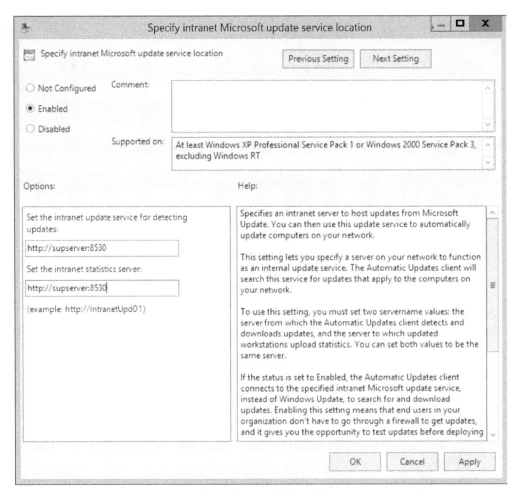

Define the Software Update Point

The preceding screenshot shows you the setting where you define the SUP server that the clients will be attached to. In the address on the preceding screenshot, you change the address to fit your environment. Replace **supserver** with your servername, as well as port 8530 if that should be different.

If you are using **System Center Update Publisher** to deploy updates from third parties such as Adobe, Dell, or HP, among other possible vendors, there is one more setting you should define in this policy.

The setting is to Enable Allow Intranet Updates.

This allows locally signed updates, published through WSUS, to be downloaded from Windows clients.

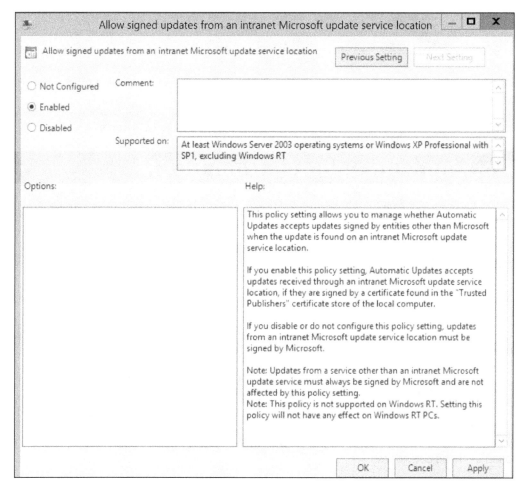

Enable setting for Allowing Intranet Microsoft Updates

You need to ensure that WSUS/SCCM is able to download updates through your proxy or Firewall, especially if you have content filtering, which many Firewalls and organizations have.

I have seen it working well and then, after a period of time, the Firewall gets new improved features that suddenly stop the downloading process of definitions.

You need to make an exception rule so that this doesn't happen.

The `PatchDownloader.log` file will not give you much, but it will give an error message as shown following:

```
Download http://wsus.ds.download.windowsupdate.com/c/msdownload/update/software/defu/2014/07/am_delta_patch_1.177.1796
Download http://wsus.ds.download.windowsupdate.com/c/msdownload/update/software/defu/2014/07/am_delta_patch_1.177.1796
Download http://wsus.ds.download.windowsupdate.com/c/msdownload/update/software/defu/2014/07/am_delta_patch_1.177.1796
Download http://wsus.ds.download.windowsupdate.com/c/msdownload/update/software/defu/2014/07/am_delta_patch_1.177.1796
ERROR: DownloadContentFiles() failed with hr=0x80072ee2
```

Basically this means something is interfering with the download phase. Have a look at this link to find what addresses you need exception rules for:

`https://technet.microsoft.com/en-us/library/bb693717.aspx`

Working with updates from SCCM

When should we use System Center as a definition source? Microsoft recommends using SCCM as your primary source for updates.

In this recipe we will cover how you can deploy the updates you need to keep Endpoint Protection updated.

How to do it...

First you need to ensure you have the categories correctly set in the SCCM site settings. These settings are forced back to WSUS. There are two categories you need to implement. They are:

- The first one is for Windows 8.1 and below and is called **Forefront Endpoint Protection 2010**. This category name will be kept for the foreseeable future.
- The second one is that Windows 10 machines are called **Windows Defenders**.

System Center Endpoint Protection will get **Definition Updates** as well as **Engine Updates** based on these categories.

So just to be clear, engine updates for all Configmgr versions (2007, 1511, 1602, 1606, and so on) will always come under the name **System Center 2012 Endpoint Protection**.

Now this can be a bit confusing, the category for update settings under **Sites** is **Forefront Endpoint Protection 2010**; and engine updates that show up in the console are called **Update for System Center Endpoint Protection 2012 Client**, even though it's for Endpoint Protection **1511** or newer versions.

The SCEP product has been rebranded as System Center Endpoint Protection. We will go through all these settings with appropriate screenshots.

First we will configure the **Software Update Point** under **Sites** components.

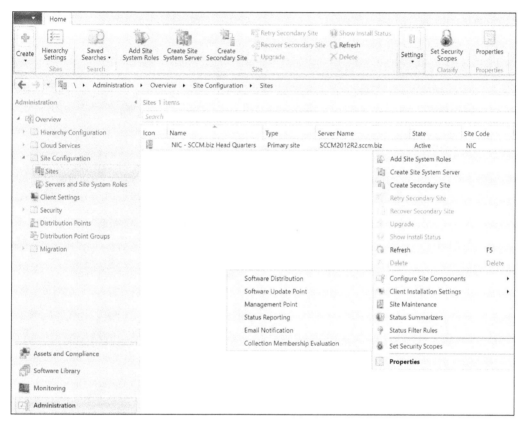

Configure Site Components setting

The settings we can define in the **Software Update Point** component are **Sync Settings**, **Classifications**, **Products**, **Sync Schedule**, **Supersedence Rules**, and **Languages**.

Remember, the settings you define here will impact all **Software Update Points** within this site's hierarchy.

For the setting following I recommend you use the default setting unless you have specific needs. This will set the WSUS server to synchronize directly from Microsoft Update.

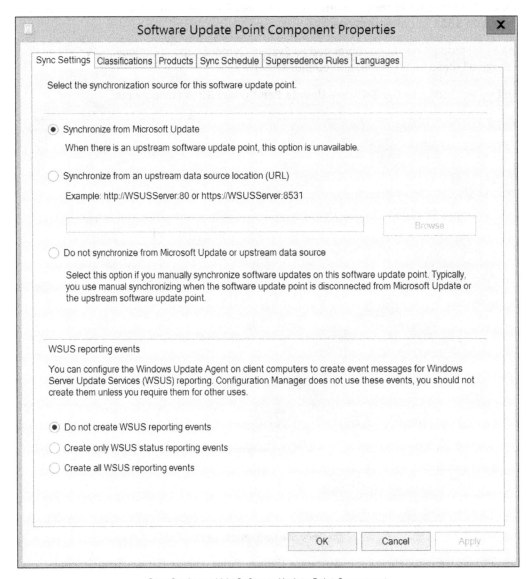

Sync Settings within Software Update Point Component

Regarding **Classifications,** I've selected the most commonly used. But you should choose those that fit your needs.

For Endpoint Protection you need to have **Definition Updates** and **Critical Updates** checked to get engine updates.

Notice that there is a new Classification called **Upgrades**. This is for new Windows 10 releases that upgrade the OS to new versions. Another tip here is to check that you have the necessary KB update on your WSUS server before you enable that checkmark. You also need to be using Windows Server 2012.

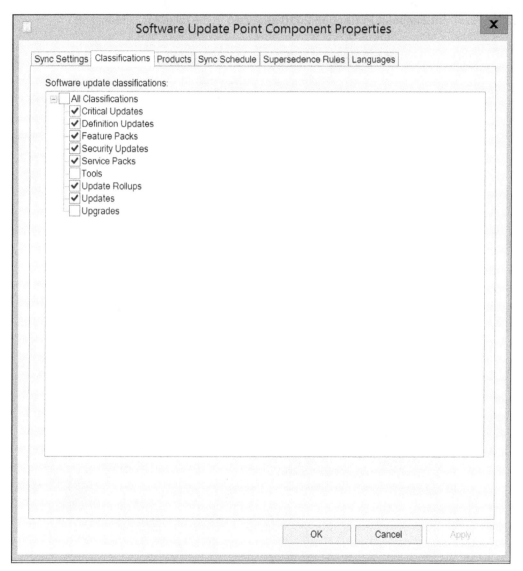

Classifications within the Software Update Point Component

We will define what actual products we want to have metadata about. This means that, when we checkmark products in this, it will not download hundreds of gigabytes of updates (it actually depends of the Automatic Deployment Rules). Taking into consideration that we have that under control, checking products here will make only those updates available for us in the console so that we can download and deploy them.

As mentioned earlier regarding Endpoint Protection, the first **Products** category we need is called **Forefront Endpoint Protection 2010** as shown in the following screenshot:

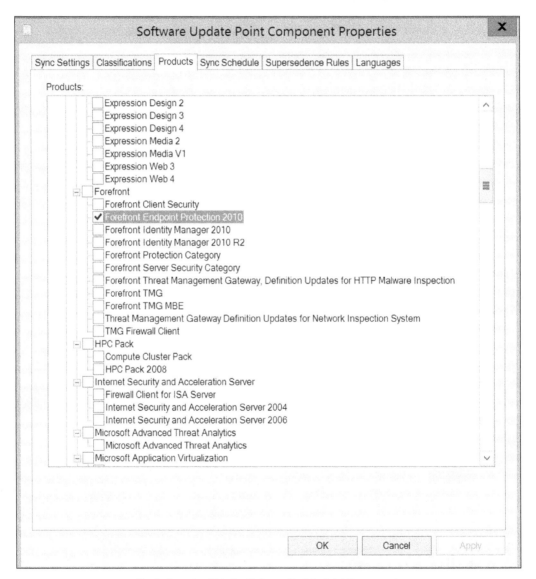

Products page within the Software Update Point Component

If or when we need to support Windows 10 machines or Windows Server 2016, we need the product category named **Windows Defender added to the standalone WSUS or Software Update Point**. This will deliver definition updates for Windows Defender that come with Windows 10 and Windows Server 2016 that SCCM will take charge of.

Windows Defender Engine Updates come with Windows 10 updates.

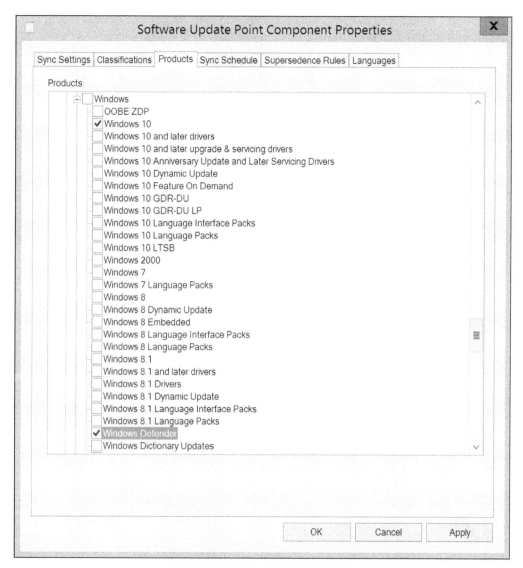

Windows Defender selection in Products

After we are done selecting **Classifications** and **Products** we need to define the **Sync Schedule**.

When we use Endpoint Protection we need to define a more intensive time schedule to ensure clients are as up-date as possible without stressing the infrastructure too much.

Endpoint Protection and Defender definition updates are released, at most, three times a day, and our server has to be told when to go and search for new content.

I recommend you set it to check at least every eight hours, which is usually sufficient. If you want a greater update frequency you can easily set it to every two or four hours instead. This depends on your environment and what business needs.

Remember to checkmark the **Alert when synchronization fails on any site in the hierarchy** as this is crucial information to know. You can also receive an email about this as we covered earlier.

Sync Schedule within the Software Update Point Component

Supersedence Rules are really more for other kinds of updates, and not Endpoint Protection.

Since Endpoint Protection uses delta files to keep new daily updates at a minimum, you will see updates quickly marked as superseded. You don't have to pay any attention to this: It's just the design and has nothing to do with the following **Supersedence Rules** setting, which will expire other superseded updates so they can easily be cleaned out.

There is also, from SCCM version 1511, an option to enable **Run WSUS cleanup wizard**. This will remove expired updates on the next **Sync Schedule if the last cleanup is older that 30 days**. Previously, you had to do this regularly yourself within the WSUS Console.

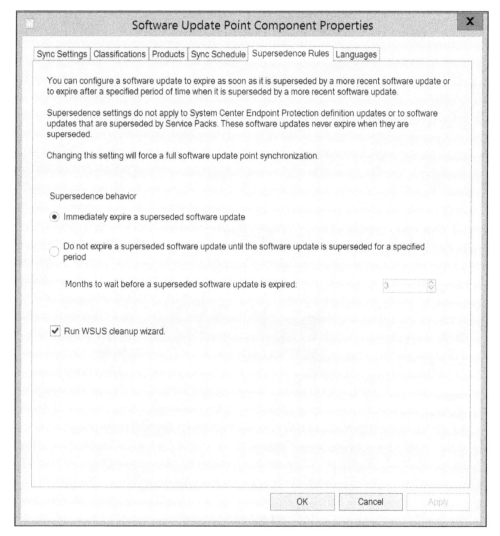

Supersedence Rules setting within the Software Update Point Component

The last step is **Languages**. I recommend keeping languages to a minimum so that Software Update metadata and downloads don't get too chunky.

Regarding Endpoint Protection, all you need check marked is **English** as shown in the following screenshot.

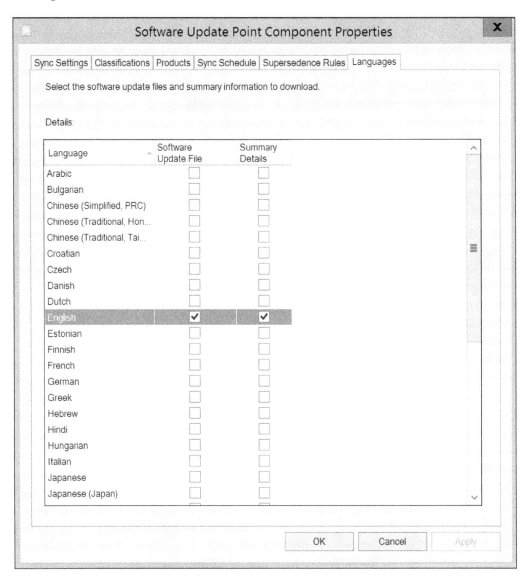

The products will now download on the next scheduled sync.

You can monitor this in the **Console** | **Monitoring** | **Software Update Point Synchronization**.

Software Update Point Synchronization status

You can also monitor the synchronization log file, which will give you more detailed information as follows:

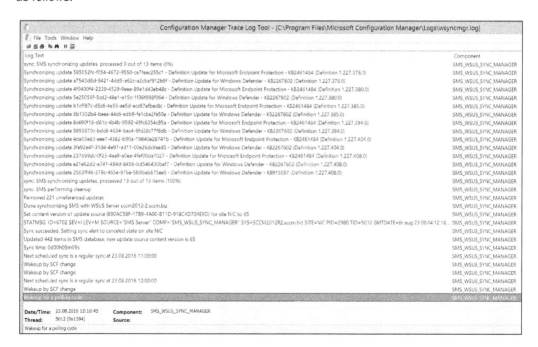

When it's finished synchronizing you can verify the sync by searching and viewing updates in the **Console by Criteria** as shown following:

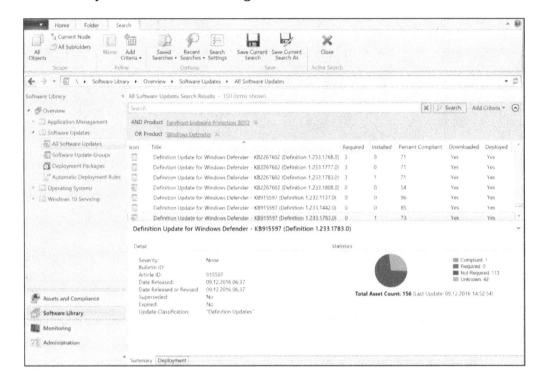

 In the following picture, we see that our Engine Updates are named **Update for System Center Endpoint Protection 2012 Client - ....**

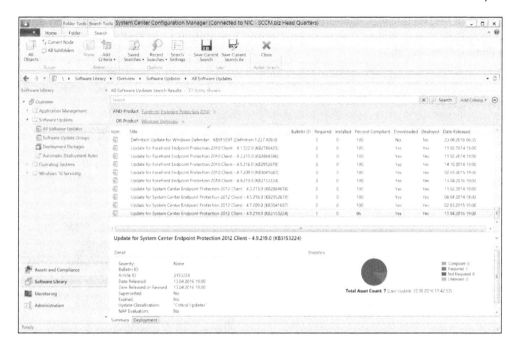

Now that we have verified that the **Software Update Point** settings are working as we wanted, we can go ahead and deploy the Endpoint Protection updates to the clients.

For that we use the **Automatic Deployment Rules**.

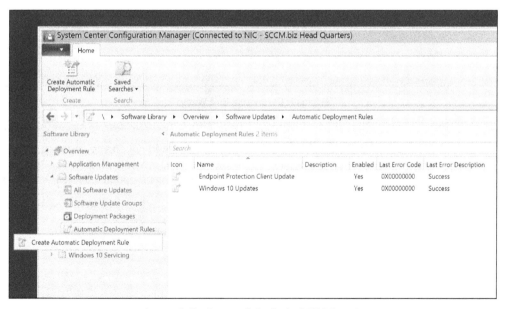

Automatic Deployment Rules in the SCCM Console

The easiest and fastest way to create an automatic deployment of Endpoint Protection and Windows Defender definition updates is to use the **Template** named **Definition Updates** as the picture following shows:

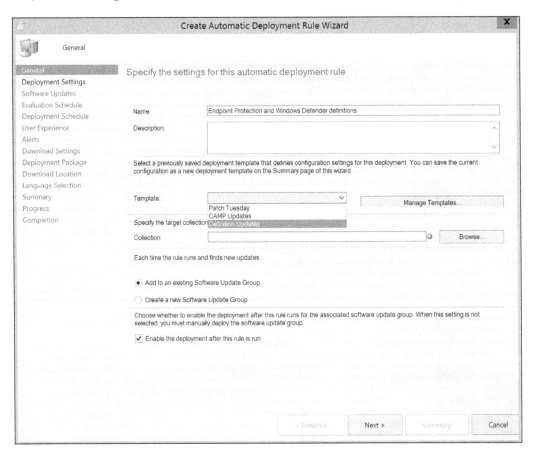

Automatic Deployment Rule Wizard

Note that this rule only deploys definition updates, and not engine updates. For engine updates you need to adjust the rule a bit: If we simply remove Update Classification the deployment will include Engine updates as well.

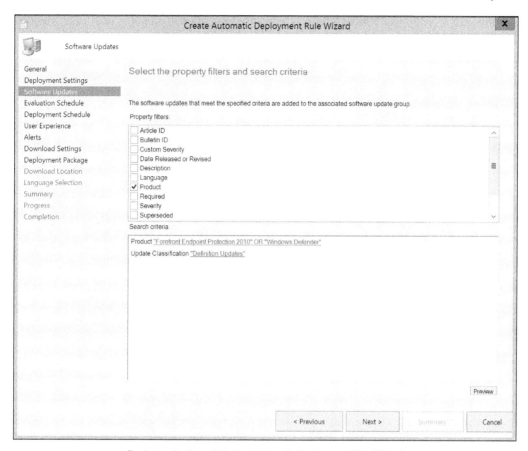

Product selection within the Automatic Deployment Rule Wizard

You can hit the **Preview** button to verify what you will get based on the settings you made.

Run the rule after any software update point synchronization is just fine, as we don't want any more delays.

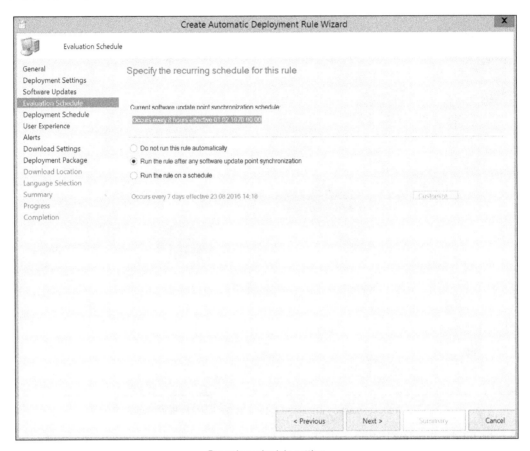

Recurring schedule setting

The default settings schedule for deployment is as follows.

The **1 Hours** setting imposes a delay so that all distribution points in your hierarchy have time to get the update before any clients ask for it. Otherwise clients may start to download the update from the possible fallback location or primary site server.

If, however, you have a smaller environment with only one location, or a very high bandwidth connection to all distribution points, you can omit the **1 Hours** delay.

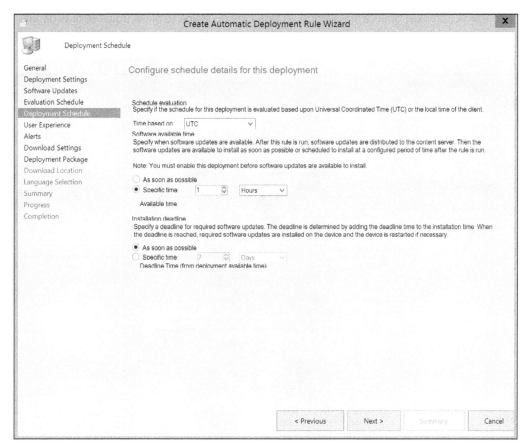

Deployment Schedule setting for this rule

Hide in Software Center and all notifications is recommended as we don't usually want to bother users with this kind of information several times a day.

I also select Software Update Installation, in Deadline behavior, to allow updates outside any defined maintenance windows. This is important to remember as we don't want any delays for these important updates.

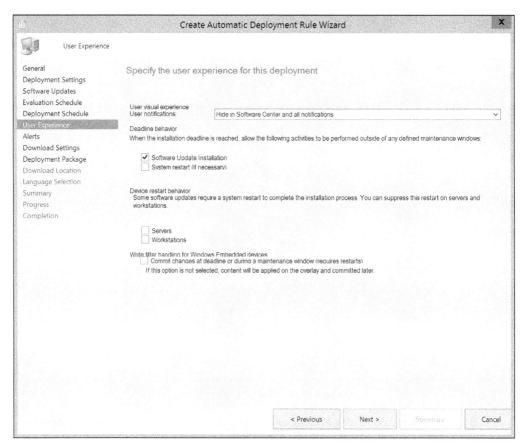

User Experience setting for this rule

I recommend you have a dedicated package for the Endpoint Protection Definition to keep it as small and tidy as possible since this is often updated.

Define it to replicate with high importance. When it comes to what collections you should deploy it to, that is up to you. I usually just deploy it to **All Systems Collection** to ensure no one is left out in the dark.

This will have no impact on systems that might not need this update if they have other Antimalware products.

There are exceptions to this: There might be situations when you have clients running another Antimalware product such as **Symantec**, which will automatically turn off and disable Windows Defender. You can get situations where Windows Updates want to install new definition updates for Defender, but this will fail because Symantec interferes with the process. This will result in a disturbing error message on Windows client machines.

If you are in a situation where you are in the process of replacing your antimalware product or you are running several products, you need to make some adjustments to both the Automatic Rules in Software Updates as well as WSUS.

Another drawback to be aware of is that the Compliance % report on the deployment job will have a lower score. However, I recommend you then use **System Center Endpoint Protection Status** view under the Monitoring tab in the console as shown following:

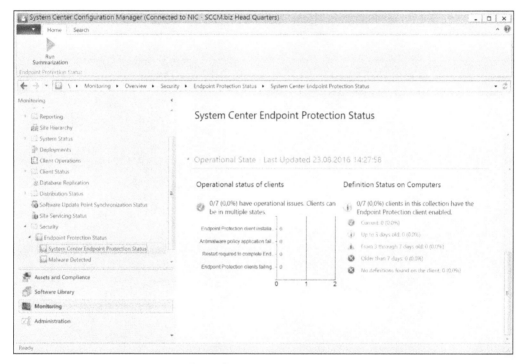

Definition Status of Endpoint Protection

What you need to consider and optimize when working with low bandwidth locations

How can we configure definition and engine client updates optimally for my bandwidth?

How to do it...

By splitting the jobs into separate rules you can limit the amount of data that needs to be transferred. You need Windows Defender and Windows 10 updates on a daily basis if you have Windows 10 clients. Also, **Endpoint Protection Definitions** need to run on a daily basis to maintain a secure environment.

However, Endpoint Protection Client Agent updates can be limited to run once a week or even once a month to further reduce traffic. There is no need for these to run several times a day.

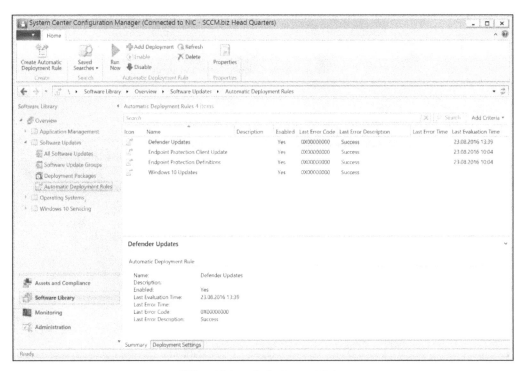

Different Automatic Deployment Rules

Remember to checkmark **Enable binary differential replication** on all the packages to reduce network traffic between sites.

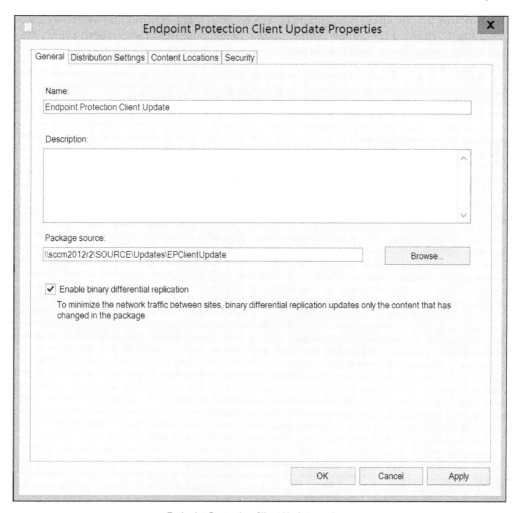

Endpoint Protection Client Update package

Why and how to use offline updates

It would be wise to have the **Universal Naming Convention** (**UNC**) share for offline updates as there might be machines with issues getting updated in the regular way.

If the Windows Update agent is corrupted or broken, then most likely neither Microsoft Update nor Configuration Manager can be used to update definitions. This is where both Microsoft Malware Protection Center and UNC shares come in. Neither of those channels depends on the Windows Update agent.

Just to be clear, though, that the Microsoft Malware Protection Center is not an offline update source.

How to do it...

You need to have the UNC update source enabled in the policy as shown following:

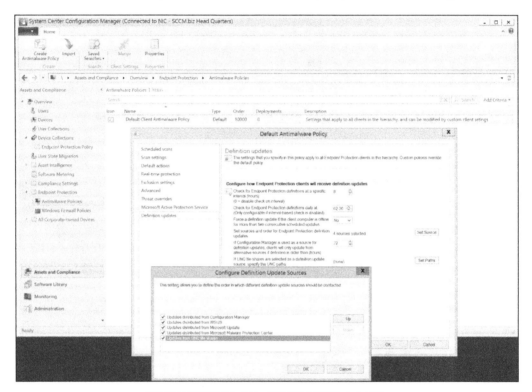

Definition Update Sources within the Antimalware policy

Then you hit the **Set Paths** button and define the server UNC shares where clients can fetch the updates.

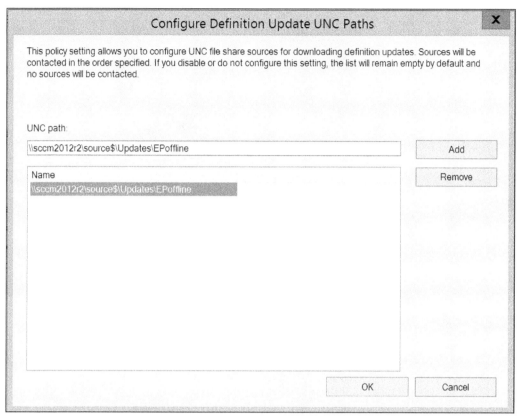

Definition Update UNC Paths

The updates can be downloaded from this address and are updated regularly:

`https://www.microsoft.com/security/portal/definitions/adl.aspx`

The picture preceding shows you the Endpoint Protection update files downloaded.

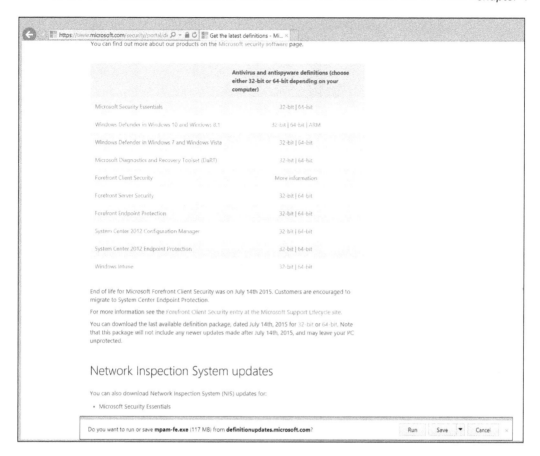

The picture preceding shows you the available offline updates that can be downloaded.

There are also PowerShell scripts that can download and execute the files for you.

One example I've seen is this, located in the TechNet Gallery:

```
https://gallery.technet.microsoft.com/scriptcenter/SCEP-Definition-
Updates-to-fde57ebf
```

It provides the option to automate the download and update process so that the files are kept up-to-date.

5

Security and Privacy for Endpoint Protection in Configuration Manager

In this chapter, we will cover the following recipes:

- Security and privacy for Endpoint Protection in Configuration Manager
- The Microsoft Security Center
- Keeping third-party applications up-to-date
- Configuring automatic sample submission

Introduction

Most antimalware and security solutions that I have seen, are often set to share whatever suspicious code or data information is found with the product solutions developer and the owner. A so called cloud feature, it's been there for years and it's actually nothing new. This gives the security product developers data to work with and to constantly improve their products. So basically it's all in all, a good thing.

When implementing and installing these antimalware solutions, they rarely or never ask you whether or not you want to share this kind of information. You might have corporate information and other reasons why you would not want to take the risk and share data.

Now sharing is a good thing, if we can make sure that the security solution we have invested in is constantly being improved.

But we should always be made aware of it so that we can make the decision ourselves. A best guess why some product leaves this default on without question, might be because people tend to leave settings at defaults and resulting that the vendor get less information surrounding the possible malware.

System Center Endpoint Protection or Windows Defender has always had this as an option you needed to enable in two different levels, **Basic** or **Advanced**.

This is because Microsoft takes privacy extremely seriously; it's a huge company and they want to be clear on when information about your environment is collected and which is not.

They do a pretty good job explaining why you should or should not enable the feature, but at the same time encourage you to go ahead and enable the Cloud feature to contribute for making the product better. The benefit for you is an enhanced real-time detection on your security solution.

Microsoft will make sure that the privacy is taken care of and that sensitive data that might contain information about a user or corporation would be hashed values, and not readable.

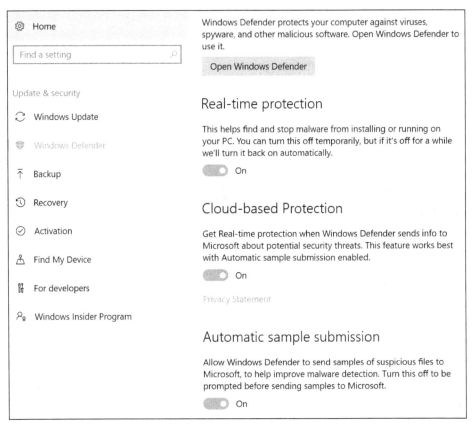

Cloud-based protection settings and Automatic sample submission in Windows 10

Security and privacy for Endpoint Protection in Configuration Manager

We know by now that Endpoint Protection uses software updates to deliver definition updates to client computers with Configuration Manager Client. With that in mind, make sure that you read Security and Privacy for Software Updates in Configuration Manager at the link following:

```
https://docs.microsoft.com/en-us/sccm/sum/plan-design/security-and-
privacy-for-software-updates
```

How to do it...

Regarding security best practice, there are a few checkpoints you will want to think through and make sure you have covered.

We have been through most of these in various aspects and how to setup and configure based on Microsoft best practice as well as my experience over the years of implementation and customer practice from real life.

I see it like this, you have Microsoft, *the developer of the product* that makes guidelines and best practice for how to setup and configure the solutions. This is based on mostly how the product works with a typical infrastructure and typical users. And then, you have the real life situation for business where you want to adapt this knowledge into a working solution securely. You have to know what settings and changes you need to do to make the solution work in your environment.

Now, the headlines and topics you need to check of are **Automatic Deployment Rules** (**ADR**). This is to make sure definition updates are automatically downloaded and approved for deployment to clients. Within this topic you have a bunch of settings both on the server side as well as on the client side. I call it server side and client side even though you configure it all on the Configuration Manager server. But configuring this poorly or misconfiguring it may lead to clients not getting daily definition updates and possible saturation of the WAN link. Now, definition updates are not huge; you can expect around 1MB a day per client. But the problem starts if you have low bandwidth connections, metered networks or a very slow satellite connections, or thousands of clients in a branch location, just to mention a few examples. So make sure you have this properly setup and configured to work in your environment, because there are very little automatic sensing in this.

Meaning the clients doesn't know how much they actually have in available total bandwidth speed to nearest Distribution Point or Internet.

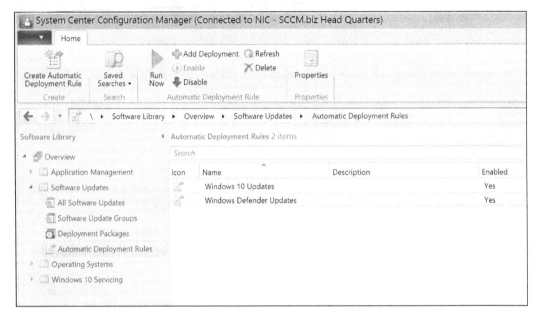

Automatic Deployment Rules in SCCM

Consider configuring All Management Points for HTTPS encrypted communication. Now, this is something I have not addressed particularly because you want to consider this thoroughly. This requires quite a lot of planning and thoughts regarding PKI certificates and so on.

 You can read more about the requirements in this Microsoft Technet link: `https://technet.microsoft.com/en-us/library/gg699362.aspx`

But why do we need encrypted communication between our clients and server infrastructure? All communication floating over the Internet today should be secured with certificate encryption. You will see this more and more in the future, but today we see it for the most part on VPNs, email, bank accounts, and websites where we need to type our login and password. So basically, it means that all communication running over port 80 HTTP is wide open for hackers and thieves to steel whatever information they could use.

The Configuration Manager client that System Center Endpoint Protection uses are mentioned in previous chapters, for deployment, policy configuration, compliance, health check, update and status reporting. All this communication will flow unencrypted on port 80 HTTP if not configured for HTTPS. Now, this is alright when the client is on LAN which is usually secured well with Firewalls and often intrusion detection. When the client computer travels home or on the Internet there is no longer any communication with the System Center Configuration Manager infrastructure. So there is basically no risk there, and this is the most common configuration in my experience. But some choose the configuration with setting up HTTPS, also called **Internet-Based Client Management (IBCM)**.

The Prerequisites for IBCM you can read more about on this link:
`https://blogs.technet.microsoft.com/jchalfant/`
`prerequisites-for-internet-based-client-`
`management-ibcm-in-configuration-manager/`

`https://technet.microsoft.com/en-us/library/`
`hh427332.aspx#BKMK_ConfigureSigningEncryption`

There is a new feature that was released with version SCCM 1610 called Client Management Gateway, that works in the Azure Cloud and allows clients to communicate with SCCM while they are using public Internet. This of course requires PKI Certificates as well as an Microsoft Azure subscription. But this is a very cool feature, and will increase the security of clients.

So what kind of communication are we talking about regarding security aspects of SCEP? This will be status messages sending information about any detected malware. If you want to council this information and are running clients in unsecure network environments you would want to consider setting up HTTPS mode for you SCCM infrastructure.

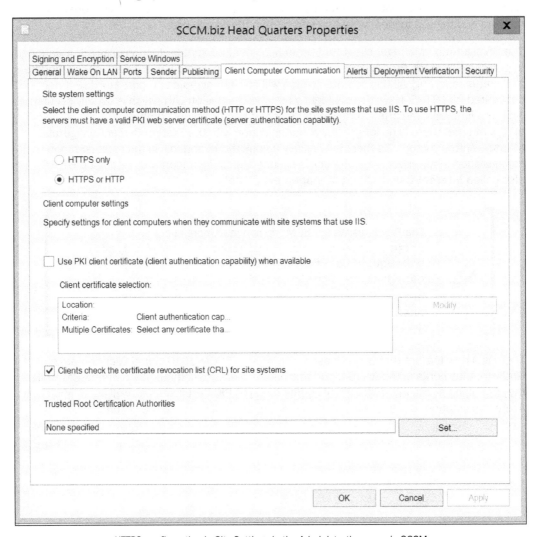

HTTPS configuration in Site Settings in the Administration pane in SCCM

Email notification: I'm sure what you would want to know immediately is whether there was an outbreak or mass spreading malware attack on your computers or servers in your business. We usually have email on our computers, phones, tablets and so on.

You should consider using a Mail Server that supports authenticated access by using the SCCM site servers computer account as authentication. If this is not possible, you should use an domain account that has the least privileges.

Avoid having users with local administrative rights as much as possible. This is something everyone struggles with, the paradox is that the larger the business is, the stricter policy they have managed to see this through and enforce it. The smaller the business is, the less strict security they have. I guess the natural explanation would be that in larger companies with thousands or maybe hundreds of thousands of users it would mean chaos and a huge security risk if every user would be allowed local administrative rights.

Even though, without administrative rights, we see that some malware like Ransomeware crypto viruses that we will discuss more in the following chapters slips through and manages to do harm. *A good policy is to always grant end users the least privileges needed.*

This is especially important when we are using Endpoint Protection, because with local administrative access the end users have the ability to do a much more, obviously. But to be more specific, they can delete reported instances of malware before it's sent to the Configuration Manager, this is done every five minutes by default. But the even more important aspect, from a security perspective, is that they can actually manage to uninstall the Endpoint Protection client and stop dependent services. Now, this is something the Microsoft Team is working on improving, called **Tamper** protection that many of its competitors have had for years. This will simply prevent others or malware from performing these kinds of harmful actions. That said, the Configuration Manager Client health check and compliance check would force the installation Endpoint Protection, but not instantly, so this is an important security aspect to think of and an improvement of this, called Tamper protection, would be very welcome in the near future.

The Microsoft Security Center

How does Microsoft Security Center work and what can it give you?

Microsoft Security Center is a Service in your Windows that monitors the security health settings, including firewall, antivirus, antispyware, windows update, **User Account Control** (**UAC**) and Internet settings. Basically all the mentioned features are related to the security of the Operating System.

How to do it...

The local service is called **Security Center** in your Windows, and it's set, by default, to **Start Automatically Delayed**, meaning it starts a little bit after the Windows has finished starting up. There is about two minutes delay, which is totally fine for several services, and will result in a more rapid Windows startup time and allowing the users to start their work faster.

 More information about the Security Center can be found at:
`https://www.microsoft.com/en-us/security/default.aspx`

Now, I have seen some companies disabling this feature, because of its alert messages to the users have become more annoying than helpful. But this was more the case before than it is now, with the new, improved Security Center in Windows 8.1 and newer. It has much better intelligence and improved detection, but you might still see this issue with some antivirus products like **Bitdefender**.

However, you may want to disable this or adjust the notification alert during a change in your antivirus/antimalware solution, because when you are in the process of uninstalling Trend, Kaspersky, Symantec or whatever product you might have, and then want to deploy and install SCEP or Defender ,the Security Center will very quickly alert the users that their computer is now unprotected and they can click here to find a solution. Now, that is not something that would definitely initiate some IT Support calls all right, but sometimes it's nice to talk to people too. But perhaps it is not something we would like at all in this matter. Since this would be something that we are now aware of, we will monitor the change of antivirus or antimalware solution with other methods.

In fact, unnecessary notifications and alerts to users are a security flaw in themselves, because in the end when there really is a security issue to take action on they just think it's some minor glitch or false alarm again.

Microsoft builds security into every Microsoft product and service, it's in their mind from the beginning to make it even more secure against todays threats. In the future, we will see a lot more applications running in virtual environments to protect the operating system layer from harmful code and exploits.

In Windows 10 it's named **Security** as you see on the picture following:

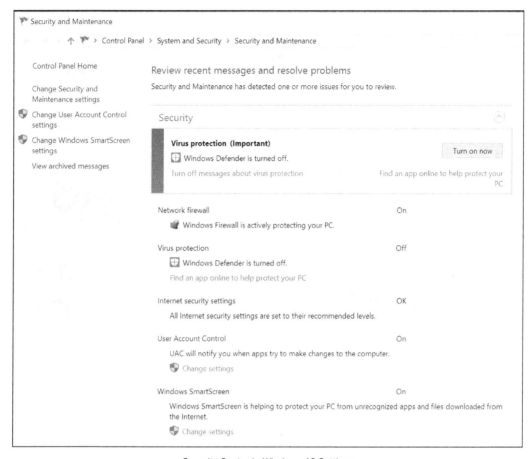

Security Center in Windows 10 Settings

Now the alert message you will see when you disable your antivirus or antimalware real-time protection is something like this:

The preceding screenshot shows you the message prompted to the user when real-time protection is turned off on the antivirus or antimalware product. This is something you would want to avoid when changing antimalware product in your organization.

Now, you can control this setting with a Group Policy, within **Computer Configuration | Administrative Templates | Windows Components and Security Center** like the following screenshot shows you:

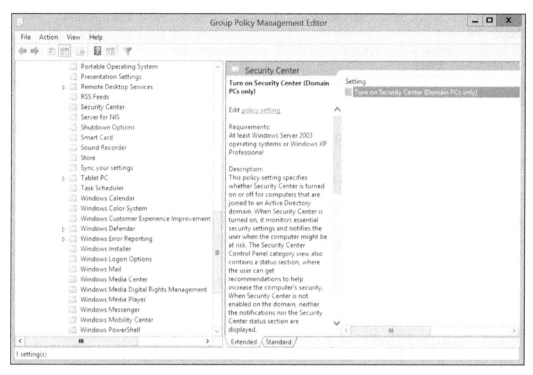

Group Policy of Security Center

Keeping third-party applications up-to-date

Keeping third-party applications up-to-date is a very important step to patch security vulnerabilities in your applications. Microsoft applications are updated through WSUS or Software Update. Next, you have the most commonly hit applications like Adobe and Java, simply because these applications have integrations to Internet Browsers.

The safest browser right now is **Microsoft Edge**.

Why you may ask? Because Google Chrome, Internet Explorer and Firefox have been on the market much longer and have far more users. Attackers simply attack were they have the largest possible impact.

Internet Explorer that comes with Windows 10 has its own Flash, and is now updated though Microsoft Updates channel. This means that you may wish to consider having a dedicated **Automatic Deployment Rule** (**ADR**) so that this product is more frequently updated than others.

How to do it...

But how to keep the old Java and the Adobe Flash Player up-to-date?

Don't forget to remove older versions of Java. If computers have both Java 6 and Java 7, it won't automatically remove Java 6 when you update Java 7. You have to deal with this yourselves.

Below are some simple command lines that you can use as an example and put in a batch file and deploy to computers. It will simply uninstall old Java versions without any further interactions.

```
UninstallOldJava.cmd - Notepad
File  Edit  Format  View  Help
wmic product where "name like 'Java 7%%'" call uninstall /nointeractive
wmic product where "name like 'JavaFX%%'" call uninstall /nointeractive
wmic product where "name like 'Java(TM) 7%%'" call uninstall /nointeractive
wmic product where "name like 'Java(tm) 6%%'" call uninstall /nointeractive
wmic product where "name like 'J2SE Runtime Environment%%'" call uninstall /nointeractive
```

A script like this may uninstall old versions like Java:

Be aware that when using the terms `like` and `%%` in collection queries, you burn more processing time on your SQL or SCCM servers. So, if you have a lot of these and plan to have that collection for a long time, you might consider more specific queries like = and with using exact name without `%`.

I often use the quick and simple way and use a Software Package for this, but you might just, with some more work, make it even smoother with the new Software Application form. This one works with very little fuzz. The users will not notice anything, and that is what I wanted.

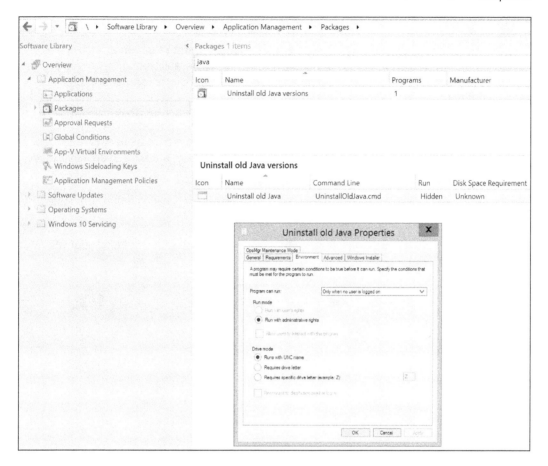

Second, I would run this with the Environment setting **Only when no user is logged on**.

This is to avoid many processes and components which are in use when the job is run and to ensure that it is more successful. You might think, *but our users never log off?*

Yes, but from my experience, if you're not in a hurry to get the job done as soon as possible, this will run eventually when the user's shutdown and reboot their machines. And yes, many users do not even do this on a regular basis. Here we touch something that I see as a big security issue, because I see computers that haven't been rebooted for two or three months and that means you're not forcing a reboot with your Software Update or WSUS Policy. This means that it's of course much more convenient and pleasant for the end users, and for the IT departments in the matter of being nice, but not when it comes to fulfill their responsibility to maintain the most secure environment possible. There is also the fact that the goal is to get more successfully application deployments too. When computers are hanging around with a lot of pending reboot on their Operating System, this interferes with applications installing. Mostly because Windows isn't securely patched before the reboot is done, the `.dll`, `.sys` files among others are not replaced with new patched files until reboot.

But isn't there a smoother way of keeping third-party applications up-to-date?

Yes, there is, you have the possibility to use **System Center Update Publisher** (**SCUP**) and several others which are far more advanced with zero-day vulnerability analysis that are undisclosed computer-software vulnerability that hackers can take advantage of. You can read more about this in the *Chapter 8, Malware Handling*.

Finally, I want to mention something that is to be considered as a good practice and a necessary safety precaution within all kinds of deployment, and it only takes a few seconds when creating the package, application, task sequence or similar. You have to specify exactly what Operating System this job is allowed to run on.

Why is this important? It may save you from accidentally targeting systems that you don't want. Like Servers, or platforms that aren't suited for this deployment.

This is very important as much as it is forgotten. I strongly advise you to set it on your OS deployment Task Sequences.

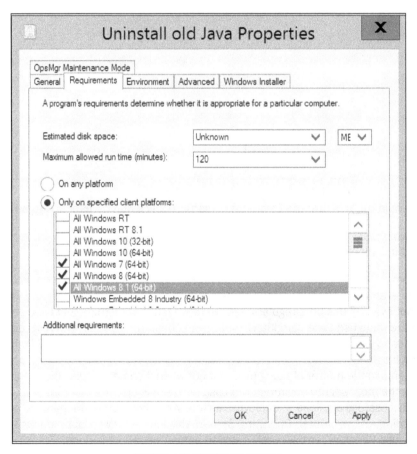

Platform selection for the program

Configuring automatic sample submission

How can I configure automatic sample submission so that my users don't have to take any actions?

Microsoft actually gets 2 million new file samples daily according to the report in September 2016, which is pretty awesome. It ensures that it's continuously improving every day. They have around 80 billion files of metadata to work with.

In the first versions of System Center Endpoint Protection, when suspicious software or malware were found, it would popup and ask the user to allow it to transfer the sample to Microsoft Cloud. There were two problems with that: first, the users got scared and called IT Support. Second, the ones who were not scared and wanted to hit the **Yes** button couldn't because they needed administrative rights.

Then the Microsoft team made a workaround with a policy that you could push out through Group Policy or in another way.

How to do it...

So, if you're still in System Center Configuration Manager 2012, you need to get this registry change out to your computers with the instructions in the link following:

```
https://support.microsoft.com/en-us/kb/3036437
```

But if you're in System Center Configuration Manager Current Branch you can skip this, because it's now very easy to configure. Well, to be more accurate, you actually need to have your System Center Configuration Manager version upgraded to at least version 1602, where the Microsoft team added this feature.

The following screenshot shows you where you will find this setting in the Endpoint Protection policy:

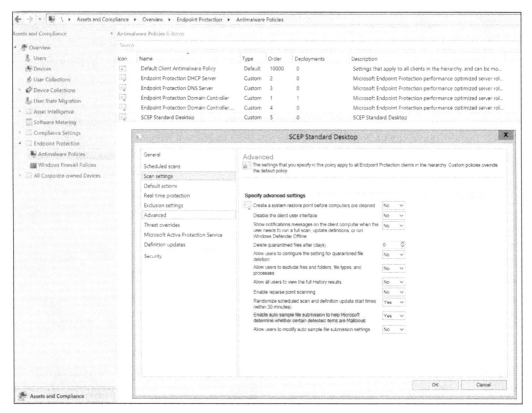

Endpoint Protection Policy where you define the Automatic Sample submission setting.

The policy is picked up by the SCCM client with the next Machine Policy cycle and applied to the Endpoint Protection agent.

Now, regarding Policy Update, many are eager to adjust this as low as possible to ensure that jobs respond quickly and effectively in the matter of what's deployed and applied to the computers.

The setting I'm talking about is located in **Client Settings** policy and called **Client policy polling interval**. This is set to 60 minutes by default when you install SCCM.

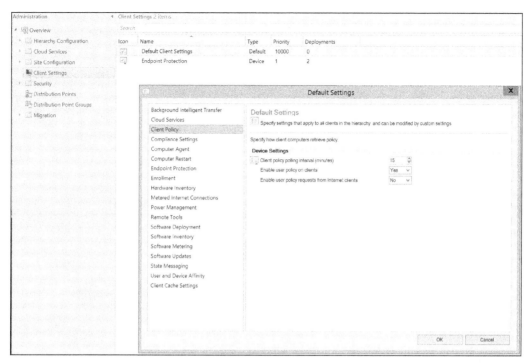

Client Policy setting

It can be set as low and often as three minutes.

However, it's strongly recommended that you reconsider setting this to a number that will suite your needs and your environment.

There are several aspects to this, one is working as latency for your own good as an SCCM administrator. Hypothetically, if you were to discover a fault or something you forgot at the last minute, you would have some time to get this right. You might be monitoring the deployment report to see how this works out in your environment. The job that you tested in the lab worked so well there, but works in a whole different manner on the computers that have a long history of applications.

Another aspect of defining another number than default 60 minutes is that lots of services and schedules within Microsoft components runs by the hour and therefor you might want to define a special minute like 47, 37 or 27 minutes, so that it's easy for you as an administrator to recognize any strange reported behavior if that where to occur. But don't set the number to low, just because you want things to happen fast. Think through all scenarios.

The second fact to this Client policy interval is that it also has a huge impact on the Distribution Points as well as Network impact. Imagine that you have 6,000 computers, and you define the Client policy interval to three minutes. You are deploying a new Office 2016 application towards all your computers. Now this would mean that roughly 2,000 computers will start to download the 1GB package from your Distribution Points over whatever connection they have more or less simultaneously. This could very easily lead to a malfunction even though the SCCM client uses the technology **Background Intelligent Transfer Service** (**BITS**).

In fact, this is also something you can define and control how much bandwidth your clients are allowed to use during work hours.

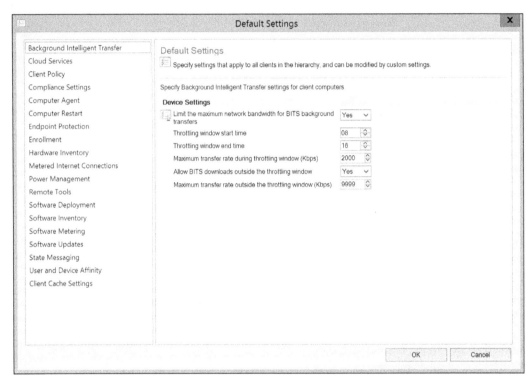

Background Intelligent Transfer settings

So imagine the impact of 2,000 computers times 1GB files on every minute.

Now, the BITS technology in itself would balance this somewhat, however in my experience the problem is very often with the virtualization environment like VMware or Hyper-V. Those kinds of virtualization, to mention the most common are superb in the way that you can utilize your Server infrastructure much more efficiently and quickly. It is very simple and quick to set up a new server within those systems and the memory, CPU, disk and network are shared very smoothly within all the Virtual Machines.

That said, the downside of this is, there is always some compromise, and that is performance. Since several Virtual Machines share the same hardware from the physical server you will have performance impact once there is a fair amount of increase in the load, whether it's this or that component. A very common issue I see, especially regarding VMware environment, is that they often are overcommitted, meaning one of VMware's great features are pushed over the limit. VMware can allow over committing, meaning it can seem to spend more memory than it actually can. This works well because very often servers don't use all the memory they claim to need. So, what might happen is that sometimes the servers actually need all the resources they thought they were given, but in reality they didn't get it and will now struggle with performance.

The end result or worse case scenario could mean that the VMware host is not even coping, or hardly breathing. You will get too many **Input/Output operations per second (IOPS)**.

Regarding SCCM, the misconfiguration of the Client Policy setting and large deployments, it could very easily lead to malfunction in your server environment and large Disk Queue length, slow response, or even situations like a host failure and shutdown. This would mean that all servers within that host will be unresponsive.

The image below indicated on a heavily used disk system, this will have slow response time and poor performance, because Disk Queue Length above 2 or 3 is considered too high, especially on a System Center Configuration Manager Server.

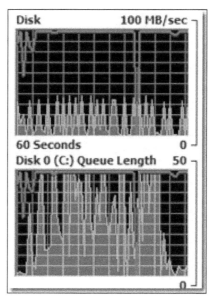

Disk Queue Length diagram from Windows Performance Monitoring

Branch Cache has been around for a while and has begun to be well known, but a new great feature released with SCCM version 1610 is Client Peer Cache. Basically, both features allow clients to share the package with each other on the same subnet but with different technologies. Client Peer Cache is newer, more advanced, and is the one I would recommend considering. These are great features that the load of the Distribution Points. It becomes more and more easy to set up and configure over time with policy and features adjusted within the SCCM Console. But you will still need some Group Policy adjustments as well, to define when the Branch Cache should trigger or not.

So, remember that the Client Pull interval's default setting of 60 minutes should do for the most part, but, depending on your number of clients, server, and network environment, you might need to configure it to 30 minutes or less. I don't recommend setting it any lower than 15 minutes.

Remember that you could very easily define different settings for different collections, so that your pilot collection could have lower interval would be a smart thing to do.

6
Configuring and Troubleshooting Performance and Advanced Protection

In this chapter, we will cover the following recipes:

- ▸ What you need to consider when running antimalware on your computer
- ▸ Configuring Endpoint Protection or Defender for Windows 10
- ▸ Integrating Endpoint Protection with OS deployment
- ▸ What you need to consider regarding BitLocker and Endpoint Protection

Introduction

Compromising on higher security often gives rise to increased complexity and reduced usability. Due to encryption, certificates, security codes, strong passwords, and malware scanning on disk or network are all factors that increase complexity and require good management solutions.

As per my experience, antimalware products that scores very high and provides high security make the machine run so slow that it's a pain to try doing anything productive on it. Then, there isn't really a good balance between performance and safety, but you want to be safe too.

With System Center Configuration Manager 1610 version, there is a new feature with Endpoint Protection named **Cloud Block Level**; this is a brand new undocumented feature that basically lowers the bar to get malware blocked. Now, this is great; it means we can adjust the protection level in the Endpoint Protection policy. So, why don't we just set it to highest protection without thinking any more about it? Well, this feature needs to be carefully adjusted and developed by Microsoft, or else we just might catch too many *False Positives*, and we don't want that either, right? But the good thing about this is that Microsoft is really working and putting their effort into improving System Center Endpoint Protection and Windows Defender capabilities to detect and fight malware. Setting this to maximum will result in blocking much more malware code, which is a good thing, but you need to be aware of the fact that it will happen to block some software that shouldn't be blocked.

However, I think Microsoft is courteous enough to inform us about this and will not enforce a big change in the feature like this. It will make it something that you can adjust by giving enterprises more control on how aggressive they want us to be in protecting them.

What you need to consider when running antimalware on your computer

We want our systems to be run with good protection, be it Windows, MAC OS, or Linux. However, it's Windows that's mostly affected by malware simply because it's the most commonly used OS and therefore most targeted.

Although there are malware, ransom malware already exist on MAC OS today and they should be protected with an antimalware solution.

Now, one thing all OS naturally have in common is that when running antimalware, they tend to get slowed down. That is the side effect of running a security product and real-time scanning for malware code on the computer. There is simply no way around this, besides making smarter and better algorithms using the smallest amount of compute power, network, and disk utilization. The same goes for the encryption of data traffic over network connections, simply to block anyone from *listening* in on the communication or tap any data, this will also slow down the speed. Because it's impossible to compress the data or at least very hard, as it uses more processing power to send and receive. Even so, I believe that in the future ahead of us all communication and data will be encrypted to be protected. Every website will be required configured with a signed validated certificate ensuring proper encryption.

How to do it...

Running antimalware on your computer may not only give the benefit of increased security, but also there are reasons such as very special software being used on computers occasionally. There shouldn't be a need for not running antimalware solution. It should instead be adjusted with the right policy containing the right settings, folders, files, and processes' exclusions to make it work properly.

As mentioned in other chapters with Endpoint Protection policy, one of the System Center Endpoint Protections advantages is that this is a Microsoft product. They know how Windows work, and they know Active Directory, Exchange, and SQL Server as many Enterprises use every day around the world.

What we will also see in the future is that more and more applications will run in virtualized environments, some kind of sandbox technology to make the operating platform less vulnerable of attacks.

However, in my experience in over a decade of many different customer environments and platforms, the System Center Endpoint Protection has done a really good job in protecting the OS with superb performance and usability. There were very few issues with running applications, windows profiles, and files open. I've experienced problems with other antimalware product to struggle with and making it painful for the end users, resulting in slow performance and delayed response when opening and closing files.

Endpoint Protection comes with readymade policy templates for desktops as well as many different Server roles for you to have a good solid starting template.

It is essential that you do the required exclusions to maintain optimal speed and proper operational function of the applications, _Especially on Servers_.

Configuring Endpoint Protection or Defender for Windows 10

Technically, there shouldn't be any difference between the System Center Endpoint Protection that comes with Configuration Manager and the built-in Microsoft Defender in Windows 10.

System Center Endpoint Protection and Windows Defender are the same. Having said this, Windows Defender will be the future branding name. It is still deployed, configured, administrated, and monitored through System Center Configuration Manager or Microsoft Intune.

How to do it...

Configuration Manager is set to administrate Windows 10 machines, which means that they get the Client Settings policy defined to enable Endpoint Protection.

Configuration Manager will only put a small management layer on top of the built-in Defender that already is in place. So, it is not similar to the process with Windows 7, 8, or 8.1 where it would in fact install the Endpoint Protection (`SCEP.exe`) file.

There is no difference in the Client Settings policy whether it's Windows XP, Vista, 7, 8, 8.1, or 10, or the Windows Server Operating Systems for that matter, but the difference is in the Definition and Engine Updates.

You need to ensure that you have your Software Updates or WSUS settings properly configured.

In products selection, there is a product named **Windows Defender** in the OS.

This will synchronize **Windows Defender** metadata definition updates to the WSUS allowing you to download and deploy them.

But be aware that you need both products Windows Defender and System Center Endpoint Protection to support all Windows platforms.

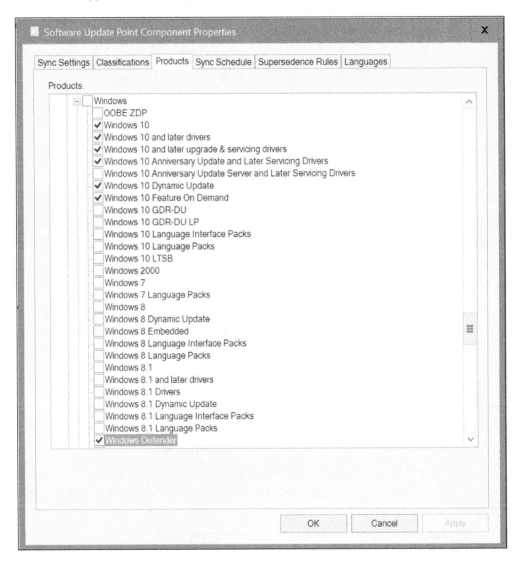

The preceding screenshot shows you the **Windows Defender** product you need to check within your **Software Update Point** settings.

Now you should also create a new **Automatic Deployment Rules** (**ADR**) or adjust it within Configuration Manager, or within WSUS if you're using that in standalone mode.

Now what about Engine Updates for Windows Defender? That will be delivered through Windows 10 OS Updates since it's so built in with the OS. This means that you should also think through your Windows 10 Update and Servicing plan.

While writing this book, System Center Endpoint Protection 1511 are close to expiration, as mentioned in other chapters, you are now on a current branch plan on System Center Configuration Manager and Windows 10 **Current Branch for Business** (**CBB**). In other words, you need to follow the continuously updated flow to be in a supported state. The Windows 10 **Long Term Servicing Branch** (**LTSB**), as it states doesn't have the same update requirements as *Current Branch for Business*, but Microsoft strongly encourages enterprises to use Windows CBB to benefit from the latest security features as well as other features.

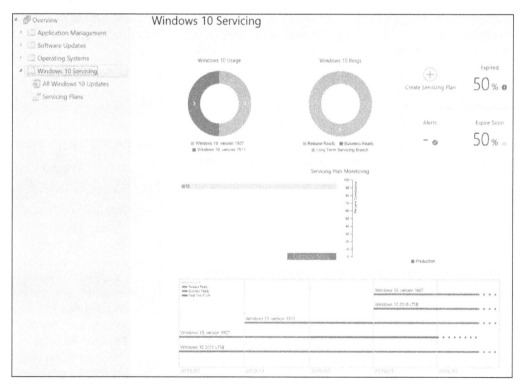

Servicing plan for Windows 10

On Windows Server 2016, we see that it has Windows Defender built-in as well, and you need to take actions on that as well, if you want to configure and monitor it with System Center Configuration Manager. The Windows Servers need Configuration Manager Client installed so that it will take control of the Windows Defender.

With this you can define policies and monitor them. This is great and very easy as it's already in place and not something you need to ensure that it gets installed right.

One of the big problems with getting antimalware solutions installed on computers and servers that have been running a while or maybe for several years is that sometimes the installation fails because there are pieces from other antimalware products left blocking. Perhaps the uninstallation some time ago didn't work 100%.

With the Windows Defender in-place from the beginning, there is a much greater chance that this will be a smaller or no issues at all in the future to come.

But the thing you need to keep in mind when setting up Windows Server 2016 is that it's there and enabled at once, so you need to make the proper adjustments so it becomes either an *Active Directory Domain Controller* or *SQL Server* so that the real-time scanning doesn't interfere with the Active Directory database or any other database. There is no automatic sensing in this.

Although if you have System Center Configuration Manager controlling these Servers you can easily deploy the correct Endpoint Protection Policy to the servers as explained in other chapters in this book.

Integrating Endpoint Protection with OS Deployment

System Center Endpoint Protection is normally deployed as a Client Settings policy, which is totally fine for existing Windows clients, by the way, but during OS deployments, this might just be something you want to be aware of. It means that Endpoint Protection is installed by the Configuration Manager Client after the OS Deployment Task Sequence is done and the client is fully working. Now, how long this takes depends on many things, such as the Windows version, network topology, latency, content and layer of the Task Sequence, and Configuration Manager hierarchy. It also needs the first initial download of Endpoint Protection SCEP Definition files that is approximately 150 MB. Now, this is usually not a problem because the OS Deployment are run toward the same Distribution Point that has the **Pre-boot eXecution Environment** (**PXE**) role and the Software Update Package that contains the definitions files. But there might be scenarios of USB sticks at locations where you would take extra considerations.

How to do it...

The problem with Endpoint Protection is it is deployed as a Client Setting is that it takes some time before the installation is enforced and kicked in by the Configuration Manager Client right after OS Deployment Task Sequence.

Now, you won't have this problem with Windows 10 since the Endpoint Protection, or, more correctly, the new Windows Defender is already in place, which is great.

But for the previous Windows versions such as Windows XP, Vista, Windows 7, 8, and 8.1 that don't have Endpoint Protection or right version of Windows Defender this will be something to be aware of.

Usually, it kicks installation in within a minute or so, but if the computer is slower or there are any other circumstances delaying it may take even longer

The danger then becomes a reality if someone shuts down the computer instantly after the Task Sequence is done, leaving Windows unprotected without proper Endpoint Protection installed. Now it will install once it gets back online on the network yes, but that might not be 100% the case every time a computer is handed to its user that just might be on his or her way to travel.

The solution to this, primarily, if you don't have Windows 10, direct access, or Internet-based Client Management setup is to create Endpoint Protection as a package and let the Task Sequence do the installation. I'm not saying use this instead of Client Setting, because that would be totally wrong. Keep the Endpoint Protection Client Setting in place as well and add this in addition.

The downside is that this package needs to be updated with the latest engine version as well to be fully updated. But it's not that big of a problem, as it will automatically be updated on the Windows computer as soon as Software Update starts working.

However, it takes some time before Software Updates and Windows Updates start working; it needs to get the policy and run its initial Windows Update scan, which is time consuming depending on what Windows platform you're on. With Windows XP, it takes a very long time, but this process gets better and better as we upgrade our OS from XP to Vista, or to Windows 7.

So how do we do this if we want to create an Endpoint Protection package?

1. The first step is to create a package that will contain all Endpoint Protection definition files.

 This part can be achieved by the following sample scripts in the links:
```
https://blogs.technet.microsoft.com/
clientsecurity/2010/09/16/using-a-script-to-
automate-unc-definition-updates/
```

However, you could also download them manually to a source folder on your System Center Configuration Manager site server and create a package from there. There are many methods and scripts for you to automate this process as well, with the help of Scheduled Task in Windows Server.

2. Create a batch file or programs for the definition updates.

3. Create the software package for the Endpoint Protection client installation. You can copy the `scepinstall.exe` and `.xml` file from your `Client` folder on your Configuration Manager site server `\Microsoft Configuration Manager\Client\`.

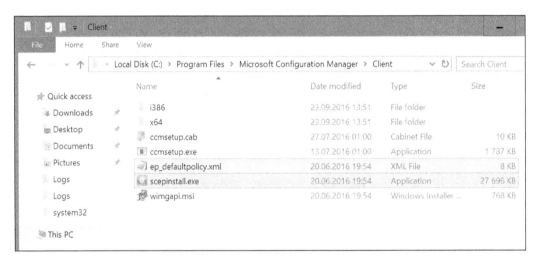

Configuration Manager Client setup files

4. The program command should be something like this:

```
Scepinstall.exe /s /q /NOSigsUpdateAtInitialExp /Policy
%~dp0EPAMPolicy2.xml
```

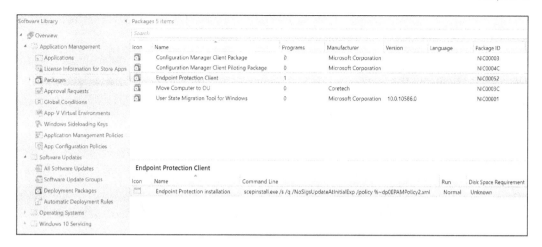

The preceding screenshot shows you the package required for Endpoint Protection Client in the Configuration Manager Console.

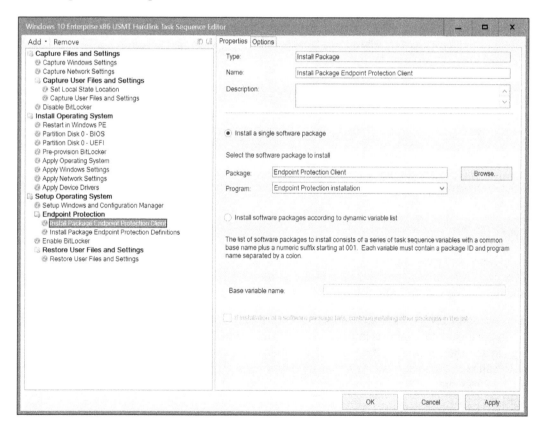

The preceding picture shows you a Task Sequence example with how you can specify the Endpoint Protection Client installation during OS Deployment.

You could also put Endpoint Protection inside your Reference Windows Image for even faster Deployment time, but the drawback is that it requires more work to keep it up-to-date.

The following link will explain more about the procedures:

`https://technet.microsoft.com/en-us/library/dn236350.aspx`

What you need to consider regarding BitLocker and Endpoint Protection

BitLocker is a security feature that came with Windows Vista; it encrypts your hard drive. The intention is to protect the data from being stolen or falling into the wrong hands. The key to unlock the encrypted drive is well-protected by a **Trusted Platform Module** (**TPM**) that Windows owns and controls.

TPM is a cryptographic, tamper-resistant module. It stores biometric data, such as the new *Windows Hello* feature that allows you to sign in to Windows by using face or fingerprint. All these features are built in to Windows.

Regarding BitLocker, the 48-digit recovery key is securely placed in Active Directory attached to the Computer object, so it's easy to recognize.

Brute-force attacks have existed for several years and are easily explained as a process that simply tries to guess the user's password, pin code, or even biometric login.

How can you protect yourselves against brute force? And what has BitLocker to do with Windows Defender?

How to do it...

Windows 7 and lower started defending themselves against brute-force by slowing down the Windows login process after multiple incorrect attempts so that you would have to wait longer and longer every time, same as you would see on smartphones today.

With Windows 10, you have an even more powerful feature and an optional form of protection when the login information is integrated with TPM. If Windows detects an attack on Windows sign-in and BitLocker encryption is enabled, then Windows can actually restart the machine automatically. When it boots up again, it will enter BitLocker recovery state until recovery key fetched from Active Directory are entered. As this password is of 48 digits, it should be pretty hard to guess.

This brute-force feature in Windows 10 can be enabled with **Group Policy** in **Computer Configuration | Windows Settings | Security Settings | Security Options.**

Named: **Interactive Login: Machine Account lockout threshold**

Value: **5**

Look at the following screenshot:

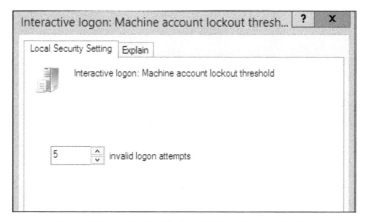

Group Policy setting for Windows 10 brute-force protection

The easy way to test if its working is to mistype your password five times, then Windows should restart automatically and you will need the BitLocker recovery key from Active Directory. Ensure that you have this information in advance because there is no way of getting back into the Windows or data any other way. That's the point with BitLocker, there is no backdoor.

Windows 10 has actually many new security features, and the production team constantly builds new features to meet today's and tomorrow's threats.

It can now actually protect against *Man in the middle* , where someone tries to reroute network communication between the user and the server, as well. Windows 10 now requires SMB signing and mutual authentication before allowing connection to Active Directory SYSVOL and Netlogon shares.

You actually need protection before Windows Defender is started as well, and that's where Windows Trusted Boot comes in verifying boot components and **Early Launch Antimalware** (**ELAM**).

If your computers have Unified Extensible Firmware Interface UEFI and Secure Boot Microsoft, strongly encourage customers to have these enabled by default. They also have security features built-in protecting the bootloaders digital signature to ensure that it has not been modified compared with its original digitally signed version. So, basically this protects against bootkits and rootkits.

With System Center Configuration Manager 1610, there will actually be a way to use Task Sequence to convert computers from BIOS to UEFI with the new Task Sequence Variable TSUEFI Drive.

Now with Windows 10, Windows Defender has got a new feature named **Windows Defender Offline** that you can initiate from within **Windows Settings | Update & Security | Windows Defender** as you see on the following screenshot:

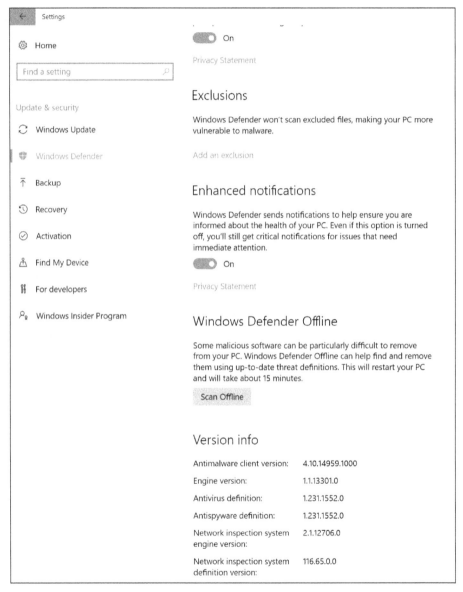

Windows Defender settings in Windows 10

To run **Windows Defender**, on earlier version of Windows you had to create a boot media with something like Microsoft **Diagnostics and Recovery Toolset** (**DaRT**), to remove malware that somehow were a bit tricky to remove because of active processes.

However, if you are running BitLocker Encryption, you have to turn it off in advance to allow scanning offline. Now BitLocker has nothing to do with malware protection, it is only encryption, so it's not in any danger that way when turned off.

Following the same procedure as when you are to upgrade BIOS on the computer, you need to suspend BitLocker while upgrading. Otherwise, BitLocker would very easily fall into Recovery mode and require the recovery key.

7
Troubleshooting and Fixing Issues

In this chapter, we will cover the following recipes:

- Dealing with Endpoint Protection issues
- Solving Endpoint Protection Policy issues
- Understanding update issues

Introduction

As with all software products, you will often encounter issues during installation or while deploying to remote systems. And often, with antimalware software, there will be challenges getting it installed and configured depending on what condition the targeted machines are in. For example, if you have hundreds, or thousands, of Windows 7 machines that have been running for several years, you will probably find that a small percentage of them have different issues in the underlying Windows services that System Center Endpoint Protection will utilize and need in order to work. Luckily, when you have a powerful tool such as System Center Configuration Manager, you will most likely be able to fix these machines without running around by sending commands, scripts, or other methods to get them repaired.

Dealing with Endpoint Protection issues

Issues with Endpoint Protection are most commonly caused by Windows services not working correctly, malfunctioning Windows instances, or perhaps other issues such as malware. For Endpoint Protection to work, it needs different services to work smoothly, such as **Windows Management Instrument (WMI)**, Local Group Policy, Windows Update, to name a few important ones. Not forgetting the System Center Configuration Client as well, which is very important and will also give you an indication of the health status of the operating system as it does a few health checks. Here, we will look into how to identify and work out some of these issues.

Getting ready

In order to accomplish this, you need to have an account that has local administrator privileges on the targeted machines.

You also need full access to the Endpoint Protection role in the System Center Configuration Manager Console.

How to do it...

Opening the **System Center Endpoint Protection Status** view in the console displays information about machines in **Different Collections**, as shown in the following screenshot. If you remember from *Chapter 2, Configuring Endpoint Protection in Configuration Manager* with recipe named *Configuring alerts for Endpoint Protection on Configuration Manager*. The list of Collections presented to you here depends on where you have deployed and enabled the Endpoint Protection policy.

Looking further, I have chosen to view all my Systems, meaning all workstations and servers. At once we spot the *red cross*, which indicates a number of active client machines at risk. This means that they fall within what the Configuration Manager security health check declares as a potential risk:

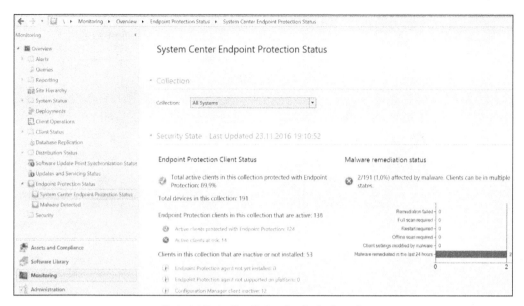

Endpoint Protection Status view in the Console

It is very important to investigate why the machines are at risk.

This is something you should do weekly in order to operate and maintain a safe environment. It is also proactive to do so, because you can solve issues before the user reports as a problem. The following are some of the problems you may encounter:

- The Configuration Manager client is not working properly

- The computer is infected with malware

- The computer already has another antimalware product installed, and Endpoint Protection is either not defined to remove it automatically, it's unsupported for automatic removal, or, for some reason, Endpoint Protection is simply unable to remove it

- The computer has very old definitions and is unable to update them

- Endpoint Protection cannot apply its configuration policy for some reason

- Endpoint Protection was not deployed and installed correctly

If we click on the label **Active clients at risk: ...**, the console will present us with a screen similar to that shown in the following screenshot, listing machines classified as at risk:

Endpoint Protection Client Status

 Total active clients in this collection protected with Endpoint Protection: 89,9%

Total devices in this collection: 191

Endpoint Protection clients in this collection that are active: 138

 Active clients protected with Endpoint Protection: 124

 Active clients at risk: 14

You will then be presented with more detailed information on every machine, together with what is causing it to be classified as a risk. Some of this information is better than other information, but usually, you will get some clue as to what you need to focus on and resolve.

Some of these errors and faults may often resolve themselves through a combination of Configuration Manager's client health-repair functions, Windows repair functions, and the fact that the user reboots the machines. If it's a malware infection that requires a reboot to do a proper remediation, this will also be resolved. But, as previously stated, you will most likely need to work out some of these on your own. Useful information in such cases could include how long it has been in this *at risk* state.

In the following screenshot, we can see that the Endpoint Protection Deployment State has a **Failed** status.

In this situation, failure is caused by **Trend Micro OfficeScan Client** not being properly removed, or at least with some component parts still hanging around in the operating system. Many antimalware products have something called **Tamper** protection as well as an uninstall password. Microsoft says that, for the automatic removal of other antimalware products to work, you should disable these functions in the phase where you replace your antimalware solution by deploying Endpoint Protection.

In the following situation, with **Trend Micro OfficeScan Client**, you could at first approach the computer to investigate and figure out how to completely remove this client software. Often, antimalware products create a small `.exe` program to remove and uninstall the product. Regarding **Trend Micro Officescan**, they place a `.exe` file called `NTRmv.exe` inside their program files folder, which you can run to remove **Officescan**. If that is the solution and you see many of these machines at risk, you could target them in a collection and deploy this removal .exe file to run on these machines.

Configuration Manager Client will automatically try to install the **Endpoint Protection** client as soon as it is able. Bear in mind that, if someone manages to uninstall **Endpoint Protection**, the Configuration Manager client will try to install it again. Otherwise, it will be reported and marked in this risk category so that you can take action. From what I've seen, this is one of the better features compared to other antimalware products:

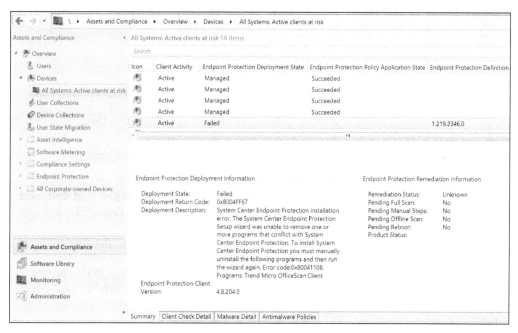

List of client machines that are in risk

If we look at another machine, such as that shown in the following screenshot, you will see that the **Endpoint Protection Deployment State** is **Failed**, but it also shows **AV signatures out of date**. To figure this out, we need to investigate further in the log files, or inspect the machine to look for symptoms. Perhaps it has a Windows Update problem:

Endpoint Protection Deployment Information

Deployment State:	Failed
Deployment Return Code:	0x8004FF83
Deployment Description:	Cannot complete the System Center Endpoint Protection installation. An error has prevented the System Center Endpoint Protection setup wizard from completing successfully. Please restart your computer and try again. Error code:0x8004FF83.
Endpoint Protection Client Version:	4.7.214.0

Endpoint Protection Remediation Information

Remediation Status:	None
Pending Full Scan:	No
Pending Manual Steps:	No
Pending Offline Scan:	No
Pending Reboot:	No
Product Status:	Service started without any malware protection engine; AV signatures out of date; AS signatures out of date

---

A computer with Endpoint Protection Deployment failure

Looking at another machine, we can see that a machine is **Active, Managed**, and **Endpoint Protection Policy Application State** is **Succeeded**, Endpoint Protection Definitions are up-to-date, and **Endpoint Protection Remediation Status** is **Cleaned**.

So, this machine has perhaps had some issues with malware and has now been cleaned out. This indicates that this machine was at risk but is no longer at risk. But you might want to pay attention to this machine if there is a lot of intermittent malware activity. You also have reports of the kinds of users or machines that are at the top of the list of activities when it comes to malware detection:

List of machines at risk in Endpoint Protection

Solving Endpoint Protection Policy issues

Policy issues are one of the most common issue I see in different business environments, especially when dealing with Windows 7 machines that have run for several years.

Getting ready

In order to resolve a policy issue on client machines, you need to have an account that has local administrator privileges on the targeted machines. You also need full access to the System Center Configuration Manager console.

You will discover that deploying System Center Endpoint Protection on your business machines will be very easy, however some of your clients will have issues that needs to be resolved. And some will actually Endpoint Protection together with Configuration Manager resolve automatically.

But why do we have these kinds of errors now, and not when I was running SCEP?

The answer is that we probably did, but it was hard to discover them in SCCM 2007 or earlier, or if we didn't have any kind of Management product.

Microsoft are good at integrating products and using existing functions and services that are already there, such as Policy, Windows Update, WMI, and so on. For Endpoint Protection, you also have the great management product, Configuration Manager, to handle it, and make sure it's healthy and working well.

Anyway, here we look further into the few clients marked **Critical** and how we can resolve some issues.

How to do it...

To identify clients with Endpoint Protection issues, navigate to the **Monitoring | Overview | Endpoint Protection Status | System Center Endpoint Protection Status**, and then click on **Active Clients at risk**.

In the **Endpoint Protection Status** view, we can scroll further down to view additional information about the **Operational Status of clients**, as well as the **Definition Status on Computers**.

When looking at **Operational Status of clients**, shown in the following screenshot, we can see that we have one client machine listed, with the state **Antimalware policy application failed**. This is the most common error I see in different environments. You need to resolve this, as otherwise clients won't get correct policy configurations about their settings.

If we want to know more about clients with this particular state, we can click on the text or count bar:

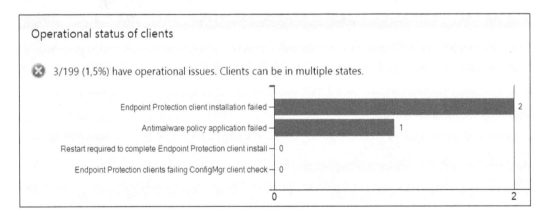

The preceding screenshot shows you the **Operational status of clients**. Click here to get more information about these clients.

After clicking the text or bar, we get presented with a list of computers based on the **Antimalware policy application failed** state, as shown in the following screenshot:

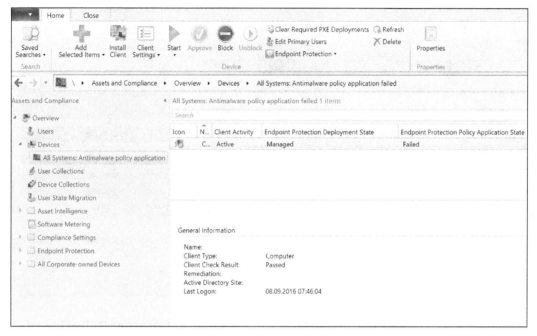

Antimalware policy application status of the machines

This machine seems to have a problem applying the **Endpoint Protection** policy.

To get detailed information on the error code and description, you can click on the pane named **All Systems: Antimalware policy application**. We are presented with this information, as shown in the following screenshot:

Policy Application State	Last Update Time	Policy Application Return Code	Policy Application Description
Failed	31.05.2016 08:50	0x80070002	Failed to trigger ConfigSecurityPolicy.exe to apply Antimalware Policy.

Error message about the Policy Application

We can also check the log file, which will display the same kind of error message for us.

The log filed is named `EndpointProtectionAgent.log` and is located in the `Windows\CCM\Logs\` folder:

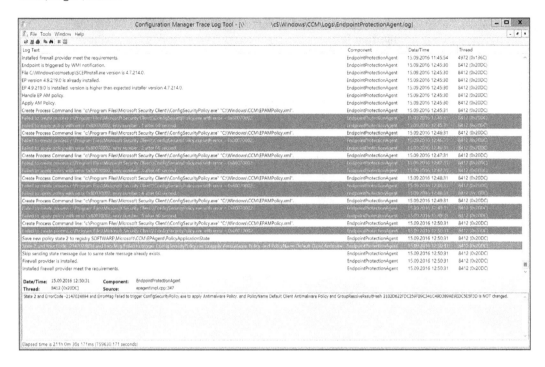

The previous screenshot shows you an example of a log file of a client computer that has an Endpoint Protection Policy issue.

Be aware that there might be multiple causes for this issue and that you might need to resolve both before the issue can be fixed. Also, if there are leftover components from previous antimalware products as well as this policy issue, you will have to solve both.

But what can we do with this policy issue?

I've often seen, particularly in Windows 7 machines, that the local machine policy is corrupt. This is placed in `Windows\System32\GroupPolicy\Machine\`, which, incidentally, is a hidden folder.

You should first try this manually on one or several machines so that you are sure this will work in your environment, but so far, I had only good experiences with this.

The `Registry.pol` file can be deleted or renamed. Windows will create a new one based on whatever local policies it may have. Often, this is none, except the one Configuration Manager client sets for **Windows Update** settings and Endpoint Protection.

After the files have been deleted or renamed, you can restart the Configuration Manager client service named **SMS Agent** and monitor the log to see if the issue is resolved.

If resolved, you should not get all the red error messages; instead you should get something similar to that shown in the following screenshot:

```
Apply AM Policy.
Create Process Command line: "C:\Program Files\Microsoft Security Client\ConfigSecurityPolicy.exe" "C:\Windows\CCM\EPAMPolicy.xml".
Applied the C:\Windows\CCM\EPAMPolicy.xml with ConfigSecurityPolicy.exe successfully.
Send State Message with topic type = 2002, state id = 1, error code = 0x00000000, and message = <PolicyName>SCEP2012 Standard Desktop
Save new policy state 1 to registry SOFTWARE\Microsoft\CCM\EPAgent\PolicyApplicationState
```

EndpointProtectionAgent.log with Successfully applied Policy

In the Configuration Manager console, when the client has reported back and the status view has updated, it should eventually change the status to **EP Policy Application State** is **Succeeded**:

Client Activity	EP Deployment State	EP Policy Name	EP Policy Application State
Active	Managed	Default Client Antimalware Policy	Succeeded

The preceding screenshot shows you the information about **EP Policy Application State** status view from Configuration Manager Console. In some cases, there will be an additional need to uninstall and reinstall the Configuration Manager client.

However, if the preceding solution should work for your environment as well, you can automate this simply by deploying a script or just deploying a command such as the following:

```
cmd /c rename %windir%\Sysnative\GroupPolicy\Machine\Registry.pol
Registry.old & cmd /c gpupdate
```

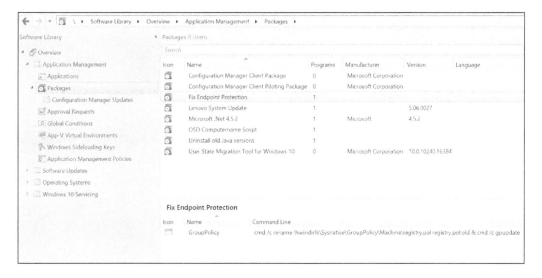

The preceding screenshot shows you an example of a command-line fix program package for `registry.pol`.

The question is, How can we target these machines with a collection?

Using this query when creating a collection, you will get machines with this state condition. This is shown in the following:

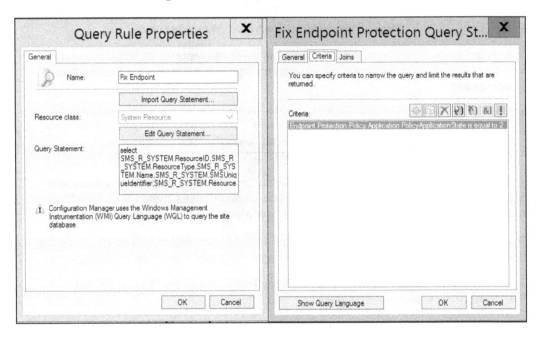

The previous screenshot shows you the collection query for Endpoint Protection with Policy issues.

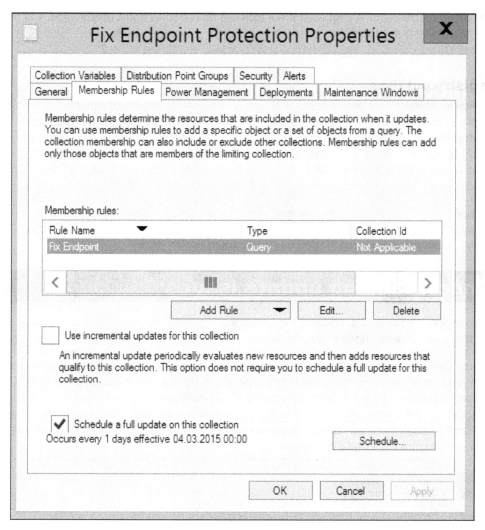

Membership rules of the Collection

I have named the collection **Fix Endpoint** because I might want to target other solutions, so that it will repair several issues at the same time.

The following screenshot shows what it will look like on the collection **Criteria** page. You don't have to use the Query text field; you could also browse your way to `Endpoint Protection Policy\Application.Policy\ApplicationState` with the value **2**:

Registry.pol files

The Administrative Templates extension of Group Policy saves information in the Group Policy template in text files with the name `Registry.pol`. These files contain the customized registry settings that are applied to the machine or user portion of the registry, which you specify using the Group Policy snap-in. The Windows 2000 `Registry.pol` file is analogous to the Windows 95 or Windows 98 `Config.pol` file and the Windows NT 4.0 NT `Config.pol` file.

Two `Registry.pol` files are created and stored in the Group Policy template, one for computer configuration, which is stored in the `\Machine` subdirectory, and one for User Configuration, which is stored in the `\User` subdirectory.

Understanding update issues

In this recipe, we will look at some of the issues found during the update process, how to deal with them, and how the update process works.

Unfortunately, it's very common to have update issues from time to time, simply because there are a lot of components involved, from Microsoft, through the Internet, through a firewall, and often a proxy for WAN optimization. Then there might even be a Network Intrusion Detection system that analyzes all the traffic going between servers. After that, it should reach your Configuration Manager defined **Windows Server Update Services** (**WSUS**), which will fetch and download the updates requested.

How to do it...

A common problem is that Firewalls or proxies may interfere with the download from Microsoft. Now, you may not have any issues with this at all, and it just might work fine. But from my experience what some businesses encounter is that over time firewalls and security features may suddenly start to interfere and block this kind of network traffic.

This is caused by security being increased with good intentions, but on this occasion it's something we don't want; we need to make sure it's working.

I recommend you take steps to ensure good connectivity without interference to Microsoft's Update source, because if this service stops, your Endpoint Protection clients will not be updated with the latest definitions and all your clients will need to use the failover mechanism and fetch updates on their own over an Internet connection.

What you need to get your Network or Firewall administrator to do is to make a pass-through rule for you, allowing the WSUS server full, uncompressed access to the Microsoft Windows Update Download addresses.

The following URL contains the addresses you need to make sure the WSUS can be reached and downloaded from:

`https://technet.microsoft.com/nb-no/library/bb693717.aspx`

If Configuration Manager Software Update Point and WSUS have issues with downloading updates, it should now show up as red in the Consoles Site Status, as well as on the first information page when you start the Configuration Manager Console, but you can also check a log file, within Configuration Managers log files, named `PatchDownloader.log`.

At first, when installing and setting up Configuration Manager, the log files are located in …\ `Microsoft Configuration Manager\Logs`, as shown in the following screenshot:

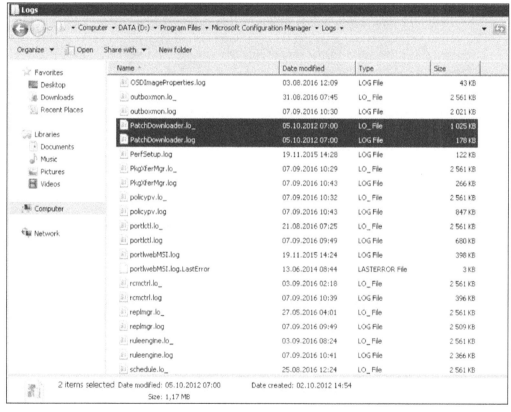

PatchDownloader.log file

After you install the Configuration Manager Client on the Site Server, it will start creating the log files in another place, ...\SMS_CCM\Logs, as shown in the following screenshot:

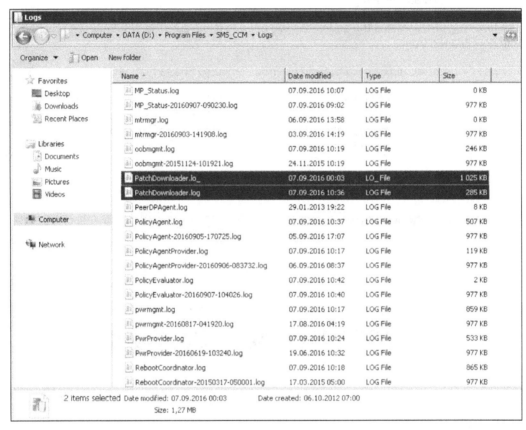

Second place where the PatchDownloader.log file can be found

This often leads to wasted time during troubleshooting because you open the first location where the log file is found, and you figure out that there has been no activity for quite a while. Therefore, you might start troubleshooting in the wrong places.

Another log file we might need to keep an eye on when troubleshooting is the file called `wsyncmgr.log`, located in the ...\`Microsoft Configuration Manager\Logs`.

This will show you what kinds of categories and updates the Server is downloading at the moment.

An example of a healthy downloader log is shown in the following screenshot:

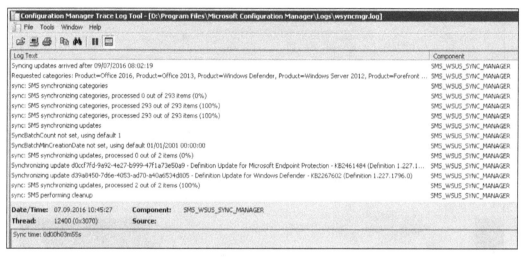

wsyncmgr.log file that shows Software Update WSUS syncronization

Antimalware Policies configure how Definition updates for Endpoint Protection are retrieved in the given order, as shown in the following screenshot.

The updates are not pushed from the SCCM server to the clients. The clients need to fetch the updates for themselves:

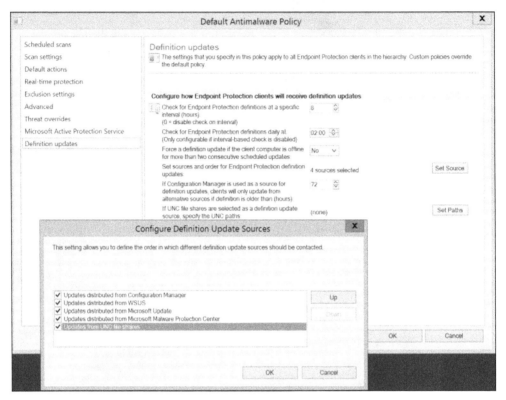

Definition Update Sources view from the Endpoint Protection Policy

Now the first three options shown in the preceding screenshot will be utilizing the Windows Update agent within the Windows component:

- From Configuration Manager
- From WSUS
- From Microsoft Update

The next two sources will not depend on the Windows Update agent, as Endpoint Protection will use its own channel to fetch updates:

- From Microsoft Malware Protection Center
- From UNC shares

Remember, as mentioned in *Chapter 3*, *Operations and Maintenance for Endpoint Protection in Configuration Manager*, in the *Creating and deploying Antimalware policies for Endpoint Protection in Configuration Manager*. For the WSUS source to work, you need to enter the WSUS Console and set up the automatic approval of definitions for Endpoint Protection and/or Defender.

Finally, we reach the Windows Client machine, which is either a Windows Server or Windows Workstation Operating System. Troubleshooting definition update issues may be very hard because of all the different time schedules and source orders, as well as the fact that very often, client machines move around on the local LAN, WAN, or Internet. Therefore, you need to pay the most attention to the update statistics in the Configuration Manager console for Endpoint Protection or reporting, as this will give you a good indication of how most of your clients are doing, and whether things are more or less as expected, based on your defined settings.

If most of your clients have not updated in the last 24 hours, this would seem to indicate a misconfiguration and/or a fault.

In the following screenshot, you will see, in the bottom-right section of the page, **Definition Status on Computers**, where there is a green checkmark named **Current**, and a number and percentage. This should represent the majority part of your client machines. Now, of course, there can be situations where most of your client machines are laptops that travel a lot, in which case, this would be normal for your business situations. Clients will update directly via the Internet, and will not report back to the Configuration Manager unless you have **Internet-Based Client Management** (**IBCM**) configured, Direct Access, or clients working through a VPN. The last two are the easiest to set up. The IBCM requires thorough planning and consideration, as well as PKI Certificates to work. PKI is also required in Direct Access, but is easier to setup and configure, in my opinion. But if you have or are planning to setup and configure PKI Certificates to your SCCM hierarchy there is now a great new feature released in version 1610 of SCCM. It's called Cloud Management Gateway and runs in Microsoft Azure, that allows you to run a Management Point, Software Update Point and Distribution Point, in the Cloud.

The cool thing about that is that clients that travel around only need an Internet connection to talk to SCCM.

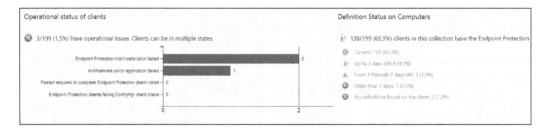

The screenshot preceding shows you the Endpoint Protection status, with focus on Definition Status.

Now, the Windows Update agent on Windows machines has issues from time to time. Fortunately, this has greatly improved with Windows 8 and later, but in Windows 7 or earlier, there were many issues where you would need to fix and repair the Windows Update agent.

When troubleshooting on the Windows client side, you would want to check a few steps.

But remember that from time to time, you would need to deploy and update the agent to maintain the clients. Otherwise, you may encounter Update scans failures and so on, causing incorrect compliance status.

The following URL will guide you in this regarding Windows 7, 8, and Server 2008:

```
https://blogs.technet.microsoft.com/enterprisemobility/2014/07/14/
how-to-install-the-windows-update-agent-on-client-computers/
```

You should pay close attention to what KB patches your WSUS Server needs, as well as the Windows Update agent on all your client computers. The Microsoft Configuration Manager Team will guide you with recommendations regarding these components.

Looking further into the Windows clients, first, there is a log file named `WindowsUpdate.log` located in `C:\Windows\`.

You need to check that the URL = http://...... points to the Software Update Point defined for that client and nothing else. This is the number-one check:

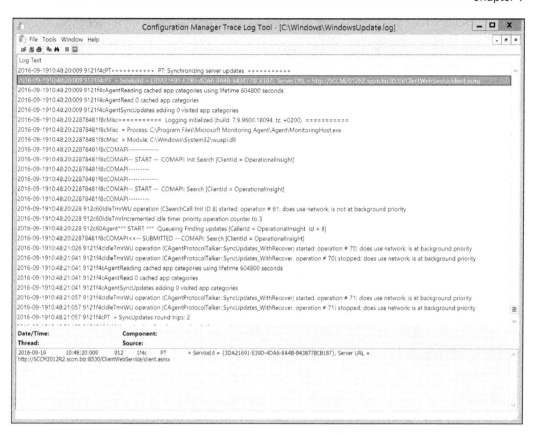

If the preceding screenshot looks correct according to your settings and environment, then have a look at the log file named `UpdatesHandler.log` located in the `C:\Program Files\SMS_CCM\Logs`.

It should indicate that it's downloading updates, as shown in the following screenshot:

UpdatesHandler.log

These are new actions you can trigger from the Configuration Manager console after updating to version 1606 or newer. You could also trigger these actions within the Configuration Manager client itself. Otherwise, you would have to wait for the client to do it based on its schedules defined in **Client Settings**.

If there is a fault with the Windows Update agent, it could be a number of things. Luckily, there are now several good solutions out there to fix and repair all kinds of issues.

An example that you might try on a machine encountering issues is this script from Microsoft Technet:

```
https://gallery.technet.microsoft.com/scriptcenter/Reset-Windows-
Update-Agent-d824badc
```

That will stop some required dependency Services in Windows Update, and re-register the necessary `.dll` files.

The end result might also be that the Windows Update Agent becomes out-of-date and does not have the correct version. Thus, it stops working and receiving updates properly.

The huge increase in attacks and vulnerabilities with Windows XP and Windows 7 demanded a large number of security updates. This resulted in the Update module reaching a maximum of 200 round trips. Microsoft is constantly working to improving this, but you need to keep your WSUS and Software Update environment as tidy as possible.

8

Malware Handling

In this chapter, we will cover the following topics:

- How to handle malware
- Responding to infections that often occur
- Monitoring infectious outbreaks

Introduction

First, it's important to understand a little bit more about the difference between antimalware and antivirus.

A virus is a written piece of code made to copy itself to the computer with the intention of doing harm, such as destroying data or corrupting the Operating System. It has been the most common threat to computer systems for the last few decades. Antivirus security products and the security patching of Windows got very good at detecting and removing this kind of malicious code from files.

So it was only natural that more and more advanced and devious ways of doing damage and manipulating computers were developed. There came an increasing need for something that could detect all of these different kinds of attacks to a computer.

Over time, software known as antimalware was developed to deal with Trojans, Rootkits, Spyware, Exploits, Worms, Adware, and last but not least viruses.

System Center Endpoint Protection or Defender will scan for and detect all of these and remove them as best it can. That is something not all of its competitors can do, though; according to the AV Test, some do better or worse than others depending on the feature in question. I think this is a very nice feature; it actually scans the software applications running on the computer to monitor and detect whether anything it finds is a good or bad application. If it doesn't recognize it and cannot determine what its purpose is, it can upload the program code to Microsoft Cloud Security Center to be analyzed there. If it's detected as an application that is actually trying in the background to download Trojans or other malicious code to the computer, it will be removed and uninstalled. This is a pretty good feature, and makes your computer safer.

Now the cool thing about this Cloud feature is that, if the Cloud Security Center determines and classifies a new pattern of harmful malware code, within few seconds the next computer searching for this kind of *unknown* malware problem will immediately get a response that this is malware.

Next the Endpoint Protection client will download the fix and take the necessary actions on the harmful software or code. All this happens in the background automatically without user interactions.

We are seeing more and more of these kinds of threats today. It could be a small piece of software hidden together with applications you're installing as an administrator of your computer. Or maybe something you click on a website, or from an e-mail. From there, attackers have a way into your computer. The malware downloads malicious code and often tries to take down your antimalware software.

It is not easy to detect whether these kinds of software application are good or bad. There is no malicious code in them, and they often seems to be just an application, such as 7-Zip, Paint, or Notepad, except that they're designed to download harmful malicious code over the Internet at a given time, or open up a way in for hackers to take control of your computers.

Rootkits are rarer, or perhaps that's because they're so difficult to detect. Rootkits basically started in Unix environments, but over the last decade they have become well established in Windows Operating Systems as well. A Rootkit actually tries to infect your machine from a deeper level and tries to hide behind the Operating System. As such, it's practically invisible. You will only notice something's wrong when the Server or Workstation starts acting weirdly, using a lot of resources, with applications crashing and the file system behaving strangely . But, compared to virus and Trojans, Rootkits are rare.

How to handle malware

How does Endpoint Protection handle different kinds of malware?

First, it's important that we understand and accept that the world is constantly changing. Everything is in flux and moving forward. With security, malware, and attacks, we have to be on a constant alert. Your security solution may be secure today, but not in a month or a year, meaning that it must be updated and kept under constant surveillance.

So the question that security admins are asking these days is, Are our computers safe and protected from malware and attacks? And what about Ransomware?

Well, unfortunately the protection isn't 100% Why? Simply because we cannot yet predict what new forms malware developers are heading towards. But antimalware products are getting pretty good at sensing harmful code. The newest and latest challenges many businesses are facing these days are Ransomware, the cryptolocker virus. System Center Endpoint Protection or Windows Defender will protect against some of these, but not all. Hopefully Microsoft will be able to fight back even against new variants of these kinds of malware.

That said, I'm not sure there is any antimalware product that will completely protect your computers from Ransom malware today. But there are few doing a better job than Endpoint Protection at the moment. This is something that everyone, I expect, is doing, constantly trying every day to improve their detection and defense.

How to do it...

Ransomware has been a huge problem over the last year now. Ransom malware starts off with a Trojan script that you get either by clicking on an attachment in an e-mail that looks trustworthy, as it appears to be an invoice or post-tracking receipt. You may also get it from a web site, but I believe e-mail has the largest impact, because it also looks like it's coming from someone you trust, or a mailing list you know.

If you don't have a very good antimalware solution for your e-mail this could easily slip through and begin its work without any warning. At this point, what it does is start scanning all your local disk drives, USB sticks, and network drives for all kinds of files. It looks especially for files that might be of great interest to you, such as documents, pictures, and data files. It then starts to rename and encrypt all the files. Then it pops up a message or alters your background picture to let you know that it has taken all your data files and encrypted them. From here on, your data files are taken hostage for money.

All you can do is to pay up or restore the files from a backup. But be sure to get rid of the malware first.

I recommend that you wipe the entire machine as you will never be 100% sure that the machine is completely clean from malware and backdoor software.

Just to give you a picture of what you might be facing, if your file system looks anything like the one shown here, you are probably infected and in deep trouble. My recommendation is to unplug the computer from your network at once.

So, is there any way we can protect our computers from Ransom malware? Yes, you can improve your protection further.

First of all, the best way is to constantly learn and instruct your employees about the dangers, what they need to be aware of, and how to operate their machine in a safe way.

As an IT admin of your company you need to ensure you have a good Firewall solution, as well as a good Antimalware solution, for your computers and server. But make sure that you don't forget your antivirus/SPAM solution for E-mail scanning.

You can benefit greatly from utilizing Microsoft AppLocker, which will essentially lock down your computers so that they can only execute a certain set of programs that you have specified.

If you have **System Center Configuration Manager** (**SCCM**) established in your organization, there should be very little need for your users to be administrators on their computers. Otherwise, this is considered a huge security risk.

As an administrator, you should offer all the software applications needed in the self-service Application portal to the users. They will be able to install them without being administrators themselves, because SCCM will handle that part from the system account.

And if a program or script needs to be run from a user or from a admin user account then that is possible as well.

So I would recommend that you remove the local admin privileges, and don't deviate from that compliance lightly.

But what about Exploits? We will return to this in the last recipe in this chapter.

Sometimes malware manages to infect Windows in a way that makes it difficult to remove while running Windows in an aesthetically and functionally pleasing way. SCEP or Defender needs to scan Windows system files offline, meaning that it will have to reboot Windows in a secure boot with very limited services running and no startup applications.

With Windows 10 version 1607 and its built-in Defender, you have the ability to very easily do this in **Settings | Update & Security | Windows Defender**.

This is something every user can do, when needed or instructed to. So far there isn't a way for admins to trigger this from within the SCCM console. To do this you need to remote a Windows 10 machine; the computer will reboot automatically after it's finished scanning. Regarding older platforms, for now you have to either use Microsoft **Diagnostics and Recovery Toolset** (**DaRT**) to create a bootable flash disc or USB to boot the infected computer on, or you need to instruct Windows to run MSConfig.exe to tell it to boot into secure mode. You can also simply press *F8* as Windows boots up.

But I would recommend having a DART boot medium available, and you might need to put some extra tools on it too. When Microsoft released version 1607, which they named the **Anniversary Update**, they significantly updated and improved Windows Defender to increase its defense against today's attacks and threats even more. Microsoft will continuously improve and update Windows Defender along with updates for Windows 10, so if you want to keep an optimum level of security, you need to keep your computers as up-to-date as possible. By creating a Windows 10 servicing plan or simply approving the upgrades of the platform, like in version 1607, and deploying that, you need to make sure that you have updated your WSUS with **KB3095113** prior to your adding the category and product named **Upgrades** in your Software Update Point settings.

What about the different Windows 10 builds? Enterprises can choose between **Current Branch for Business** (**CBB**) or **Long Term Servicing Branch** (**LTSB**). One should really think this through. From a security perspective the recommendation I would give you is to plan and go for CBB, with LTSB as Plan B. What I mean by that is that LTSB should be used for client computers that have very little need to stay current with the latest releases, features, and updates. Those machines will probably just stay on the Local Area Network, and work very little on the Internet. They will most likely not be laptops traveling around and plugging in to all kinds of networks. Therefore, CBB will be the most secure platform release to stay on, but will require more rapid servicing and updates from the administrator.

Another rule of thumb is that, if you plan to deploy Microsoft Office to your machines, you most likely need the CBB version of Windows 10.

There are several huge components within Windows 10 that Microsoft constantly works to make more secure, while also working to improve their performance and usability. Its comprehensive threat resistance consists of a combination of Windows Firewall, Windows Defender, Device Guard, Microsoft Edge, SmartScreen, and Office ATP. Office **Advanced Threat Protection** (**ATP**) requires Enterprise E5 licensing.

SmartScreen actually blocks around 97% of all known threats trying to breach Internet Explorer and Microsoft Edge. Another thing to keep in mind when running SCEP or Windows Defender is that the interactive module for the Internet browser does not work on all kinds of system. Does my SCEP or Windows Defender scan downloads before they are run or not? It works very well with Internet Explorer and Microsoft Edge, of course, and also with Google Chrome, but it does not work in Mozilla Firefox. So if you're running Firefox in your organization, be aware of this issue.

Microsoft Edge is currently a less attractive target to attack with its available vulnerabilities than other well-known browsers.

That said, how do we handle malware?

From my experience, System Center Endpoint Protection and Windows Defender, in most cases, find malware on their own, and require very little work or attention from the administrator. It does not bother the user or the admin unnecessarily. This is great, as we don't want a lot of unnecessary warnings and alerts if it's considered not to be a great risk for the environment. As mentioned earlier in previous chapters, you can define on what level you want to be alerted in the Console and e-mail alerts.

Perhaps you do want to know about all the detected malware so that you can be very well informed about what's going on, and for peace of mind.

Often, however, administrators have several roles and responsibilities in the company, and they only want to be alerted about critical stuff. They don't want to be bothered otherwise.

Perhaps you might consider having different levels of alerts. For example, if Malware is found on certain servers such as Domain Controllers, Exchange Servers, and other important servers, you need to be aware of this, because then there might be someone who is operating a bit carelessly. I would strongly advise an admin to not use a Domain Admin's account, or an Administrator of the domain to not download content from the Internet or for that matter do any Internet browsing with a Domain Admins rights account. For security reasons, you should rename the Administrator default account for the domain. It is still possible to figure this out if you are clever, but it's slightly more hidden from potential attacks. The password should be strong, long, and difficult, and the account should not need to be used.

Large enterprises use delegation between **Organizational Units** (**OU**) and delegate needed rights to Admins. For Group Policy Management, you might want to look closer at **Advanced Group Policy Management** (**AGMP**) in the Microsoft Desktop Optimization Pack. You can refer to it in the following URL: `https://technet.microsoft.com/en-us/windows/mdop.aspx`.

With the AGMP you will gain more control and security with whatever changes are made in the Active Directory Group Policy. Admins that edit and create Group Policies need to check in the policy with their user, and policies can be rolled back with ease if something has gone wrong. You can have admins that approve it before it's applied, but the most important thing to remember is that it's all logged so you know what and whom to go and see. Another benefit is that the `admx` template content files are stored centrally and only need to be updated and added once.

But what can we do with malware that is found by System Center Endpoint Protection or Windows Defender?

If we first take a look at the Console in the Monitoring section, we can see what's found and how it's automatically handled.

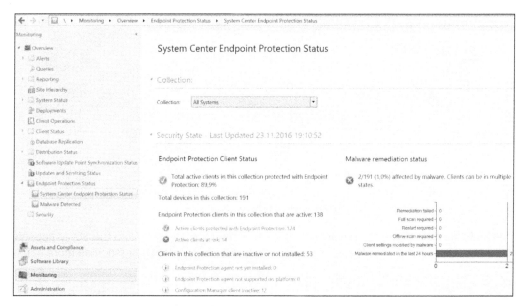

System Center Endpoint Protection status

As you see, to the right of the screenshot, we have **Remediation failed**, **Offline scan required**, and **Client settings modified by malware**. Those are areas we need to pay attention to. We don't want to see a lot of machines in those. But so far, over the past years and across different environments, I have not experienced many computers in these categories, and that is good. It means that SCEP and Defender are doing their job and protecting computers from being infected very well.

But the area on the left, **Active clients at risk: ..**, is nearly never at a zero count. We have covered this topic in the previous chapter, and it is important for you to deal with.

A good rule many companies have implemented is that *if they have a computer constantly infected with malware, they notify the user of it, and mostly, on 9 out of 10 occasions, they just reformat the disks and perform a fresh install*. It's much less work to do this when you have a System Center Configuration Manager OS deployment in place.

Also on the same System Center Endpoint Protection Status page we can easily monitor the top 5 types of malware based on the number of computers that the malware is found on. This will give us good information about the most common types of malware our business computers are encountering right now. The following screenshot shows you an example of this:

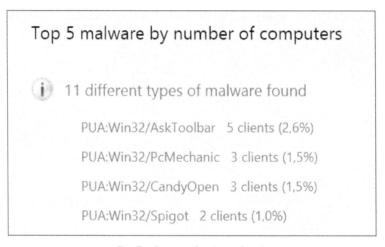

The Top 5 types of malware found

You can figure out the user that was involved in the malware infection from the SCCM console very easily. Usually the user also gets a heads-up in how to operate their machine more safely.

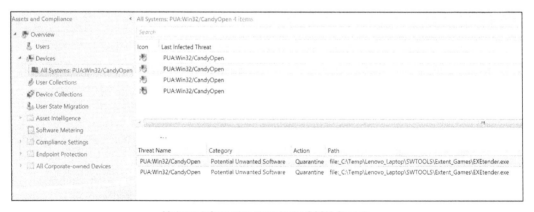

Malware information given in the SCCM Console

Another benefit of just wiping the local disks of the infected machines is that you never know for sure how deep the infection is and what else could be there, hidden.

A dangerous situation is where the Domain Admins log on to a machine that a user reports as having trouble. Perhaps it is running slowly, cannot log on correctly, has applications that keep crashing, or windows that pop up occasionally. Perhaps the user has also ignored malware information messages. The Domain Admins log on and this is where the malware snaps the login information and benefits from the Admins login credentials to spread itself among the infrastructure.

So, therefore it's important for you to gain as much information through the SCCM console as possible, and try to resolve the issue remotely, before you find the need to take physical action on the infected computer.

The actions you have available within the SCCM Console are a **Full Scan**, **Quick Scan**, or **Download Definition** for one machine or several machines.

Endpoint Protection actions you can set in action.

The action you will most likely be using is **Full Scan**, if you encounter a machine that is troublesome and repeatedly discover malware on it.

But as has been said, if it often or continually pops up malware warnings, you will probably want to wipe it and re-install Windows.

Users should be instructed to store important work on server locations so that nothing is lost if the machines are broken, stolen, or infected. To prevent your laptops as well as Workstations from being physically stolen and corporate data lost to criminals or industrial espionage, you might benefit from using Microsoft BitLocker. It's fast, safe, and easy to use. As you probably have seen as an SCCM admin, you can set it and enable it on appropriate computers with SCCM. But just to be clear, BitLocker does not protect your data from Malware, Ransomware, or any similar programs. It protects your data from being physically stolen if you should lose your computer or it is stolen. With BitLocker enabled, the data on the local hard drive is safe if someone should try to break into it and try to extract the data. You would need the pin code and password to enter a Windows OS that owns the **Trusted Platform Module** (**TPM**), which has the decryption key to open the files on the hard drive.

You might want to learn as much as possible about the malware in question. Now, you don't have to remember the correct name and Google it. All you have to do is hit the button; Microsoft has made this available for you within the SCCM Console.

The previous screenshot shows you buttons and information available for you in the SCCM console when you click on a client machine.

When you hit the button named **Malware Detail**, you are automatically presented with a web browser that immediately takes you to the Malware Protection Center at Microsoft.

This will present information you need to know about the malware, and you can easily Google more information from there if needed.

The preceding picture shows you the Malware Protection Center that the SCCM Console button **Malware Detail** presents to you. You might need further manual removal instructions if there are some infections that SCEP and Defender does not manage to remove by themselves.

But remember to try an offline scan as well. With the cloud feature enabled, you might see that it will be resolved later on, as Microsoft has treated this new malware in the cloud and the clients are downloading removal instructions for it.

See also

If you manually want to submit a sample of some files that you want Microsoft to investigate, upload it at the Malware Protection Center page: `https://www.microsoft.com/en-us/security/portal/submission/submit.aspx`.

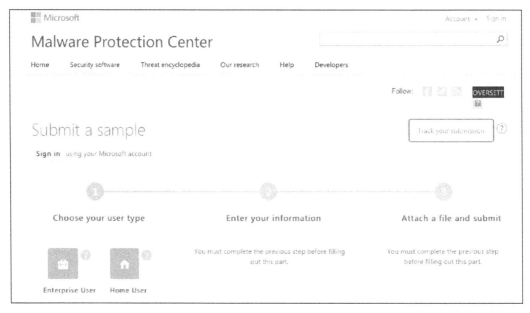

Malware Protection Center

Responding to infections that often occur

Microsoft is making Windows more and more secure every day. This is a huge focus for the developer team, because a security risk for one person is a security risk for all. Time, money, information, as well as trying to be as productive as possible are all challenges that we must face. It's no secret that there is more malware developed to target Windows than other platforms, because it has a massive user target area.

Your business needs to be using the latest possible platform to be as safe as possible; these platforms are where the largest corporations, unfortunately, will have to use more time and money to keep up.

The result of that is they have to have even tighter and more secure environments, using strong firewalls, passwords, two-factor authentications, locked-down file systems, encrypted disks, memory sticks, locked-down USB ports, and so on. Then we have the ability to lock down and control all applications we want to allow running on the computers. This is very effective security-wise, but of course has its cost when users want to go beyond that restriction. Microsoft solved these issues by developing AppLocker.

This is something that has been around since Vista and the 2008 server, and all you have to do to get it working is to configure a Group Policy.

Implementing this has been shown to have a huge benefit in increasing security.

Getting ready

You need access to the Active Directory Group Policy, with the rights to create and edit Group Policy objects for your computers.

You need to test this out on a few computers before you put it into a site-wide policy for all your computers.

How to do it...

If you have Office 365 you could make this policy in the Azure cloud. Within **Mail Flow on Exchange** you simply create a new rule to block EXE files.

Software Restriction Policies are an older technique originally designed for Windows XP and Windows Server 2003 to limit applications that require administrative rights on computers.

And with years of experience Microsoft developed AppLocker with Windows Server 2012. You can easily configure and enable with Group Policy, which is what all Admins can start doing in their Enterprises today if they have your licensing in order. It depends on your Windows client licensing, as it does with using BitLocker.

Now, to prevent your computers from getting Ransomware while utilizing Software Restrictions, the first step is to create a Group Policy to test an **Organization Unit** (**OU**) in the Active Directory that will block or prevent `*.exe` files that reside within the Local App Data store of every computer from running or starting.

Now you need to do some testing around this, because there might be an application that needs to run executable files within AppData, such as Java and Adobe, and then you need to make exclusions for those.

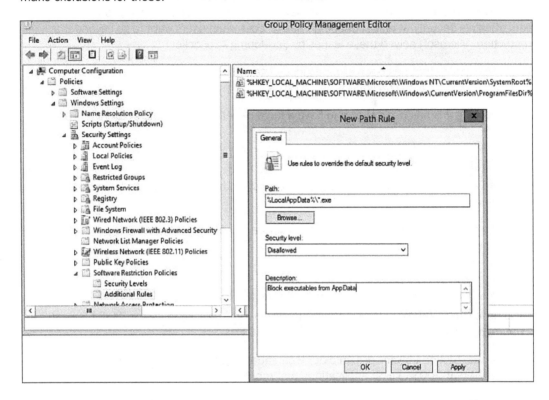

The preceding screenshot shows you the rule for Software Restrictions that will block *.exe files from **LocalAppData**.

An method that Firewall admins often use is to block everything, and then open up those that need tests to be run.

Then the newer AppLocker feature will work in another way, namely, we block everything but whitelist the applications we care about and want to use.

The fastest and recommended way to go ahead with this is to have a reference machine that is fresh, clean, and basically the way you want every machine to be. You can then access it with Group Policy Management, as the following link describes, which will automatically generate executable rules for you, and will result in a finished Group Policy for you to apply in your organization.

Of course this must be tested, and, like everything else, it needs maintenance every time there is a change. But it gives great security, and will most likely prevent Ransomware in the future.

See also

- You can read more about Software Restrictions Policies by following this link: `https://technet.microsoft.com/en-us/library/hh831534.aspx`

- For more information about AppLocker, visit this page:

  - `https://technet.microsoft.com/en-us/library/ee791835(v=ws.10).aspx`

  - `https://technet.microsoft.com/en-us/library/ee619725(v=ws.10).aspx#BKMK_SRPdifferences`

Monitoring infectious outbreaks

If you don't want to go as far as implementing AppLocker as described in the preceding recipe, there is another method that you can consider.

We will look into how to protect your computers with more tools than System Center Endpoint Protection will give you. We will be looking at scenarios for the **Enhanced Mitigation Experience Toolkit** (**EMET**).

Another possibility that we can investigate is simply blocking certain file extensions that all known cryptolocker and ransomware programs use, such as `.locky`, and `.zepto`. Later in this chapter I will show you how you can achieve this.

How to do it...

First, **Exploits** need some explaining.

These are vulnerability holes in software installed on computers. Malware can slip through the antimalware solution and then has the ability to take advantage of and use these vulnerabilities to exploit how the software works; it can then figure out a way to infect computers concealed from the antimalware software.

This is an increasingly common form of malware attack these days, and you need to know how to handle it and protect your computers in the best way you can.

We have all read or heard about security vulnerabilities with Java and Adobe Flashplayer, to mention the two most affected software programs.

Why are these more exposed than others? Is it because they are weak and poorly built? No. It's simply because those applications are, globally, the most installed software , and therefore they have a huge potential as a target. It is also a fact that these kinds of application are not updated frequently enough, and the attackers take advantage of this.

So, in other words, the best way to protect your computers from Exploits is to keep them updated as rapidly and frequently as you can, if possible, by simply keeping an eye out for when there are new versions available, and downloading and deploying them.

I would also recommend using the free **System Center Update Publisher** (**SCUP**), or another third-party product that can integrate into SCCM. These cost money, but will give you more important features as well. There are several good alternatives that will also give you a live heads-up about malware risks, such as Secunia Patch Management.

It's also important that you keep all your other Microsoft software up to date with WSUS or Software Update.

A good tip that you could do right now is to *go to your console in SCCM and do a search in Software Updates for whatever product updates computers require but you haven't deployed.* Do this now, and you might just be surprised to find out that you left out something in your **Automatic Deployment Rules**.

But what if we want to protect our workstation computers even more from Exploits? There is a Microsoft Toolkit named **Microsoft Enhanced Mitigation Experience Toolkit** (**EMET**). This is a supplemental security defense tool to protect potential vulnerable applications.

It's free and works on all supported Windows platforms, and Microsoft recommends it particularly for Enterprise customers to protect applications running on old platforms, such as Windows XP, as this Windows version has huge security deficiencies compared to the newer Operating Systems.

Another tip for you to keep in mind is that 64-bit versions of Windows are more secure than 32-bit ones; in fact, the EMET security features are more comprehensive and work better on a 64-bit platform as well. There is also the fact that many kinds of malware do not work so well with 64-bit, so my suggestion to you is that *when your organization is doing an OS deployment to a new release, consider always making it 64-bit* by checking all applications, printers, integrations, and hardware drivers. One other point is that 64-bit Windows requires at least one additional gigabyte of memory more than 32-bit versions.

The sad part when dealing with the OS upgrade is that you cannot upgrade from 32-bit to 64-bit; not even with the Windows 10 upgrade in place, which is simply a fantastic piece of work. You have to do a new fresh install. No other Windows upgrade has been more successful in my opinion. Now you can even upgrade Windows Server successfully. But I recommend that you do that with great care and with a full backup in advance.

EMET has been there for several years now, but maybe not everyone has heard about it. The current version uses no fewer than 12 mitigation techniques to detect and block Exploits, which will make it harder for attackers to find a way to infect your computers. Most of these techniques are very much involved in protecting memory from corruption, such as data execution prevention, mandatory address space randomization, and structured exception handling.

You can download EMET from this link, and you can control and deploy Group Policy to handle the configuration in your Enterprise: `https://www.microsoft.com/en-us/download/details.aspx?id=50766`.
EMET User Guide: `https://www.microsoft.com/en-us/download/details.aspx?id=50802`.

The following screenshot shows you the options you have when installing EMET:

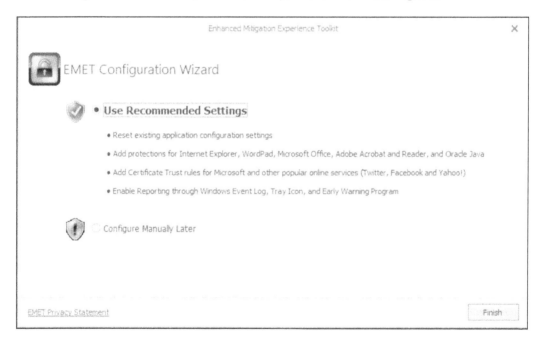

The following screenshot shows you the EMET GUI and the applications it has found installed on the computer:

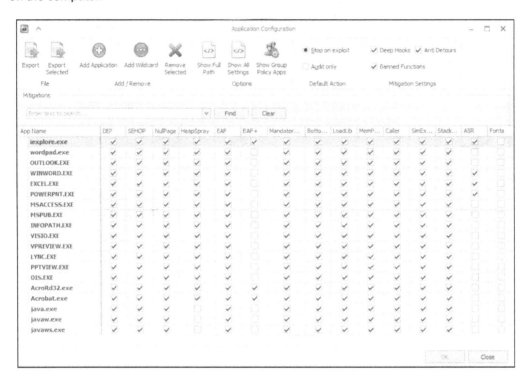

If an application is being blocked by EMET for whatever security reason, the user will get a message box like the one following:

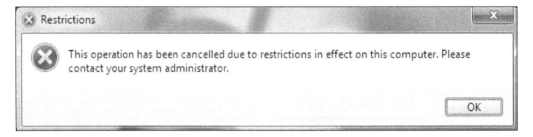

The following settings are the default EMET settings. **Data Execution Prevention** (**DEP**) is, as you can see, set to **Application Opt In** or **Application Opt Out** for maximum security. But be aware that this may prevent applications from working properly. I would recommend you try this with care and not on a mass scale. Leave it set to the default, or create opt-out rules for applications that will simply not work with EMET. Another great feature is **Audit only**, which will only log events, so you can monitor them better before starting to secure and block.

The preceding picture shows you the default settings for the EMET GUI. The events are logged by EMET to the application log in the Windows Event log.

With this you have the ability to monitor using System Center Operation Manager or another monitoring solution that connects to the Windows Event log.

Power BI is approaching the standards of SCCM, Intune, and Windows 10. It is really neat for the Administrators to put up on a big screen to give you important information specific to your environments and needs; it can clearly display, for example, the Windows Update status of my clients, or how my deployments are doing, or my antimalware status, or my current EMET attacks status, and so on.

This is the kind of information that is easy to forget about, given that you only look at it when something is wrong. But what if you could prevent huge faults, errors, outbreaks, and attacks by having a better monitoring solution or a good Power BI view to keep a daily eye on it all?

Would there be a risk if I look away from it for a while?

Well let's say you have a user who receives a suspicious e-mail; just by clicking once on the e-mail with the preview pane on the right, the computer gets infected with an Exploit malware. This could very well be a Ransom malware, encrypting all the user's data files.

If you are using BitLocker, be aware of this. When implementing EMET, you need to suspend BitLocker. There have been issues with this, so please follow the suggestions by running some PowerShell commands and then follow the further instructions shown in this article at Microsoft: `https://support.microsoft.com/en-us/kb/2458544`.

I think we will, in the near future, see that more and more apps will be running in virtualized environments, so that malware will not be able to cause so much harm to the environment and Operating System.

Protecting the Windows File Server from known Cryptolocker malware

It is important to make clear that this solution will only block known file types. We know that Cryptolocker will try to rename the data files to a given file type name extension, for example `.ZEPTO` or `.CRYPTO` to mention a few.

So, it's vital that the Server will be updated with new file types in future. But by doing this right now could prevent your business data from being lost, and save yourself a lot of work.

The following PowerShell Script will work on Windows Server 2012 or newer versions. It will install the Windows feature named File Server Resource Manager if it's not already installed.

```
---------
$a = gwmi win32_logicaldisk -filter DriveType=3 | Select -ExpandProperty
DeviceID

install-windowsfeature -name FS-Resource-Manager -IncludeManagementTools

Import-Module Servermanager


New-FsrmFileGroup -name "CryptoWall" -IncludePattern @("*.ecc","*.
ezz","*.exx","*.zzz","*.xyz","*.aaa","*.abc","*.ccc","*.vvv","*.
xxx","*.ttt","*.micro","*.encrypted","*.locked","*.crypto","*._
crypt","*.crinf","*.r5a","*.XRNT","*.XTBL","*.crypt","*.R16M01D05","*.
pzdc","*.good","*.LOL!","*.OMG!","*.RDM","*.RRK","*.encryptedRSA","*.
crjoker","*.EnCiPhErEd","*.LeChiffre","*.keybtc@inbox_com","*.0x0","*.
bleep","*.1999","*.vault","*.HA3","*.toxcrypt","*.magic","*.
SUPERCRYPT","*.CTBL","*.CTB2","*.locky","*.zepto")

foreach ($i in $a){
```

```
$Notification = New-FsrmAction -Type Event -EventType Warning -Body "User
[Source Io Owner] attempted to save [Source File Path] to [File Screen
Path] on the [Server] server. This file is in the [Violated File Group]
file group. This file could be a marker for malware infection, and should
be investigated immediately." -RunlimitInterval 30

New-FsrmFileScreen -Path "$i" -Active: $true -IncludeGroup "CryptoWall"
-Notification $Notification

}


$a = gwmi win32_logicaldisk -filter DriveType=3 | Select -ExpandProperty
DeviceID

install-windowsfeature -name FS-Resource-Manager -IncludeManagementTools

Import-Module Servermanager

;New-FsrmFileGroup -name "CryptoWall"

New-FsrmFileGroup -name "CryptoWall" -IncludePattern @("*.ecc","*.
ezz","*.exx","*.zzz","*.xyz","*.aaa","*.abc","*.ccc","*.vvv","*.
xxx","*.ttt","*.micro","*.encrypted","*.locked","*.crypto","*._
crypt","*.crinf","*.r5a","*.XRNT","*.XTBL","*.crypt","*.R16M01D05","*.
pzdc","*.good","*.LOL!","*.OMG!","*.RDM","*.RRK","*.encryptedRSA","*.
crjoker","*.EnCiPhErEd","*.LeChiffre","*.keybtc@inbox_com","*.0x0","*.
bleep","*.1999","*.vault","*.HA3","*.toxcrypt","*.magic","*.
SUPERCRYPT","*.CTBL","*.CTB2","*.locky","*.zepto")

foreach ($i in $a){

$Notification = New-FsrmAction -Type Event -EventType Warning -Body "User
[Source Io Owner] attempted to save [Source File Path] to [File Screen
Path] on the [Server] server. This file is in the [Violated File Group]
file group. This file could be a marker for malware infection, and should
be investigated immediately." -RunlimitInterval 30
```

```
New-FsrmFileScreen -Path "$i" -Active: $true -IncludeGroup "CryptoWall"
-Notification $Notification

}
```

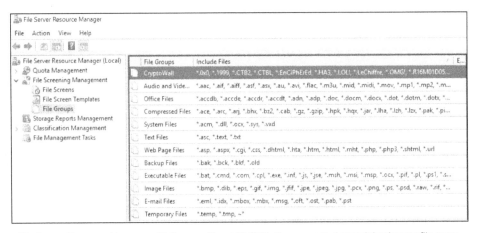

PowerShell Script after running successfully on a Windows Server 2016

Now we have managed to install the File Resource feature and defined the File Group rules with known `Cryptolocker` file types. No guarantees are given with this; you must ensure that the file types don't conflict with your environment and needs.

File Server Resource Manager with the new *CryptoWall* File Group created containing known file types.

As you can see from the script, we have only enabled Notification alerts if any of these file types are created on `Drive C:\`.

You can view notifications in the Application log from within Windows Event Viewer.

So, we don't block anything yet.

The next step is to define a File Screen Template **CryptoWall** and, as you see in the following screenshot you need to define a **File screen path** to whichever folder or drive you want to block these file types on, and choose the **CryptoWall** template.

You can modify the preceding PowerShell Script if you want to automate this last part, and run it on several Windows Servers.

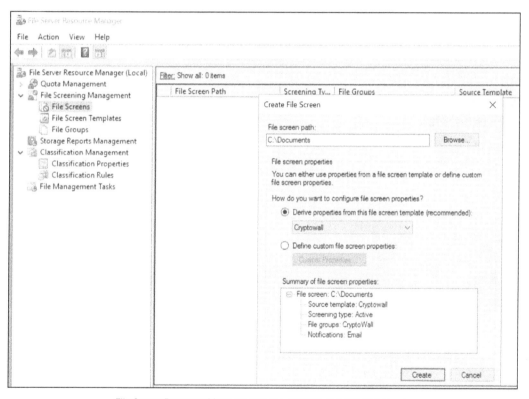

File Server Resource Manager with the creation of a File Screen rule

Another smart thing to do is to set up and configure Email alerts on this, so you know if there are any outbreaks or attempts. You configure this within the same console in the File Server Resource Manager.

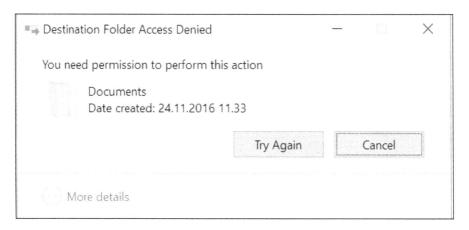

When you try to create a file with any of those file type extensions, you should receive the previous message.

That's it!

Index